1,00

‖‖‖‖‖‖‖‖‖‖‖‖‖‖‖‖‖‖‖‖‖‖‖‖‖

☑ **W9-BCQ-552**

3 1168 03068 9205

Multnomah County Library

Books are due on the latest date stamped below.
Fines are 10¢ per day for adult materials; 5¢ per
day for juvenile materials.

APR 1 3 1991

MAY 1 8 1991

AUG 2 0 1991

FEB - 4 1993

F-CIRC-02
06/89

12/96

ONE
SHINING
SEASON

ONE SHINING SEASON

MICHAEL FEDO

PHAROS BOOKS
A SCRIPPS HOWARD COMPANY
NEW YORK, NEW YORK

First published in 1991.

LIBRARY OF CONGRESS CATALOGING-IN-PUBLICATION DATA
Fedo, Michael.
One shining season / Michael Fedo.
p.   cm.
Includes index.
ISBN 0-88687-608-7
1. Baseball players—United States—Biography.
2. Fedo, Michael. I. Title.
GV865.A1F43   1991
796.357′092′2—dc20
[B]   90-7944
CIP

Printed in the United States of America

Pharos Books
A Scripps Howard Company
200 Park Avenue
New York, NY 10166

Jacket and book design by Bea Jackson

10 9 8 7 6 5 4 3 2 1

For my grandson, Cameron Frolik,
who is still young enough to entertain the dream
of playing professional baseball.

CONTENTS

PREFACE

In 1950 my younger brother, David, then seven years old, read twenty-two books to win a reading competition at Grant Elementary School in Duluth, Minnesota. His prize was a book of his choice. He didn't know whether to select an illustrated biography of Abraham Lincoln, a book of puzzles called *The Junior Whiz*, or Jack London's *White Fang*. He asked me for advice.

I had recently learned that there was a publication by Hy Turkin and S. C. Thompson called *The Official Encyclopedia of Baseball*. It was a thick tome, which our parents never would have purchased and we could not have afforded ourselves. I pressured David to ask for that book, for I had, within the past couple of years, become fascinated with the numbers and statistics of baseball. I routinely computed all the averages for all the members of the kid teams I played on. I usually led my teams in hitting, because I indeed batted well, and because, as unofficial scorer, I used to credit myself with base hits when fielders' choices were called for.

To own a book containing the records of everyone who had ever played in the big leagues, to be able to pore over endless statistics, would be for me a prize beyond compare. David seemed leaning toward *White Fang*, and probably would have picked it, had I not convinced him that it would make him terrified of dogs. Reluctantly, he was persuaded, and we got the encyclopedia. David never did crack its cover, but I virtually wore it out over the next half-dozen years.

Baseball continually fascinates many of us in ways other team sports can't. Much of this fascination has to do with strategies and numbers—percentages, averages. Because baseball is so numerical a game, it permanently marks everyone who has played it—especially those who have made it to the major leagues.

Anyone who has ever appeared in a ball game at the big league level is a statistic. He has done something in a game that can be measured. A National Football League player who played only on special teams for a game or two and who perhaps never made a tackle figures in no statistics except number of games played. Nor does an offensive lineman rack up numbers. A solid defensive basketball player may not attain data for steady play unless he manages steals or blocked shots. But a baseball player who has batted in the big leagues faced a particular number of pitches, was unsuccessful or successful in reaching base, maybe stole bases, scored runs, made plays in the field. Numbers have always figured importantly in baseball, and modern statisticians continue to come up with new definitions and numbers which, while seeming to trivialize baseball, really add to the rabid fan's involvement with our national game. It would seem that no one but a baseball manager or diehard enthusiast could possibly care about a player's batting average with runners on first and second base when there are two outs and the count is two-and-one. Yet such data are accumulated by athletes' agents and factored in when they are making contract demands. Data may also be held against a player who has not performed well. And all of this contributes to our continuing intellectual interest in baseball.

Those of us so addicted to baseball probably began our involvement at an early age. My first baseball memory dates to my second birthday. I am sitting on the living-room floor upstairs in the duplex where my mother, father, and I lived on Regent Street in Duluth. My father is kneeling several feet from me, holding a baseball bat and softball. I am wearing a regulation-size fielder's glove on my left hand. He lightly taps the large ball with the bat and it rolls slowly over the faded mauve carpet, stopping when it bumps my glove. "You caught it," my father yells excitedly. He retrieves the ball and taps maybe three or four more rollers my way, and I think he says, "Way to go, Mickey. That's my little ballplayer."

The glove, bat, and ball were his presents to me on my second birthday. In reality, he would use the glove himself for play in the softball league he routinely led in home runs during the early forties, the war years. I would take it over later in 1947, when I was eight, the glove well broken-in and supple, its golden leather exterior a much darker, richer brown where my father had formed a pocket. The leathery pungency of that glove filled the small closet in my room where I kept it, and in the many idle moments when I'd lie on my bed listening to ball games on the radio—usually *The Mutual Game of the Day* with Al Helfer—I'd be thwacking a ball into the pocket.

More than that, though, I used the glove as an eight-year-old right fielder for the Central Field Cadets; we won the city twelve-and-under championship that year. I was by far the youngest player on that team and batted leadoff. Opposing pitchers, perhaps feeling sorry for our team for having to use so young and little a player, would lob a slow first pitch down the middle for me. Infielders would creep halfway to the plate, and outfielders would assume the positions vacated by infielders. Invariably I managed to hammer a line drive into the outfield for a double. Next time around, pitchers would not ease up, but that didn't matter. I was mature beyond my years as a batter, and I hit the good pitches too.

One time that year, a team in the fourteen-and-younger division was short a player for a league game and recruited me for right field. They were as amazed as the opposition when I went six for six.

Those were heady days for an eight-year-old who was just beginning to read major league box scores and newspaper profiles of Ted Williams, Joe DiMaggio, and Stan Musial. I made our local paper myself with my hitting heroics and was starting to tell people I wanted to be a big league baseball player when I grew up.

This infatuation continued well into and beyond adolescence. I remained what one coach called "a good man with the bat" through American Legion and high school play. I batted left-handed, and rarely saw a curve ball because there were few decent lefty pitchers in Duluth. I never batted below .400 during my boyhood career, and the dream of pro ball continued. I knew my throwing was of the scatter-arm variety, but, geez, how many guys have lifetime .400 averages? I expected—but never received—calls and letters from major league scouts.

Lloyd Claveau, the elderly manager of our American Legion baseball team, thought scouts were prejudiced against us because we lived in the far north and wintry springs delayed the start of our season into late May or even June. "They figure because our season is short, we just can't develop good baseball players," Mr. Claveau told me.

This probably was true. At that time, only two area natives had ever made it to the big leagues: Dick Wade, whose father, Frank, owned the local Class C Northern League franchise, got up for a cup of coffee with the 1923 Washington Senators, and Morrie Arnovich, from Superior, Wisconsin, just across the St. Louis River bay, once made a run at the National League batting title, hitting .324 for the 1938 Phillies. Hall-of-Famer Dave Bancroft, second baseman for John McGraw's old New York Giants, also lived in Superior for many years, but wasn't born there. Even if we claimed him as our own, he really didn't develop as a player there. So scouts weren't likely to pay much attention to a kid from the northern hinterlands, even a kid with gaudy statistics.

But Mr. Claveau wrote a letter on my behalf to the Chicago White Sox, whose Northern League affiliate was now the Duluth-Superior Dukes, suggesting they take a look at me in light of my two consecutive .400-plus seasons. They agreed, and a trial was set for me at Duluth's Wade Municipal Stadium when the Dukes returned from an Aberdeen and Sioux Falls, South Dakota, road trip.

Joe Hauser, a minor league home-run slugger of Ruthian stature during his playing days at Minneapolis in the American Association, was the Dukes' skipper. On a chilly June morning he put me through paces with a scout named Johnny Mostil, whose claim to fame was that he was the only center fielder in major league history ever to catch a fly ball in foul territory. Hauser and Mostil directed me to go out by the scoreboard in left center field. Each man had a fungo bat and two balls. One would hit a ball toward the left-field foul line and I'd race for it. No sooner would I pick it up and fire it back than another ball would be on its way to center field. All the while Mostil's raspy voice urged, "Get after it, son."

Within minutes the taste of blood rushed into my throat. I thought I might stop breathing, though I could still hear the persistent Mostil shouting, "After it, boy."

I saw the concrete fence before me in left field. The ball

bounced once on the warning track and hit the wall. Weak, and stumbling on legs of sponge, I didn't bounce on the warning track, but rather off the wall, unable even to raise my arms to protect myself. I woke with abrasions from head to shoulders, and the voice of Johnny Mostil saying, "You gotta get those if you want to play in the big leagues, son."

I did not play in the big leagues, nor even in Class D. My dream died with that dive into the fence at Wade Stadium. I probably wasn't good enough anyway. I may have been among the best in my neck of the woods, but that was nowhere near good enough for pro baseball. My only brush with organized baseball occurred a couple years later when the Dukes hired me as public address announcer at $5 a game.

I suspect my dream of playing professional ball was really not much different from that of many kids of middling talent who starred in amateur or semipro leagues. Yet making it at any level in the professional game is a major achievement, and making it all the way to the big leagues is even more significant. It is perhaps almost statistically impossible. Since the official inception of baseball records was begun in the 1870s, fewer than 13,500 men have made at least one appearance in a major league game.

Because of its extreme inaccessibility for the overwhelming majority of us, we pay inordinate homage to those who have succeeded in attaining the major leagues. They are, many of them, our heroes of youth and even adulthood. In them we see what we would like to have been, and perhaps what our children and grandchildren may yet become. And if we have seen them play, they are timelessly etched in our memories as perfection in the bloom of young manhood: Joe DiMaggio's flawless, effortless swing; Ewell Blackwell's right arm, a whip snapping a fastball toward home plate; Brooks Robinson rifling a ball to first after scooping a bunt barehanded; Henry Aaron watching home run number 715 clear the left-field fence. Though these men age with the rest of us, their accomplishments do not, and they achieve, therefore, a sort of immortality. And by appearing in even one major league game, a man achieves a touch of the immortal. His name and his age, his position and his batting and fielding data go into the record books, and there will be a file on him in the Hall of Fame at Cooperstown, forever.

But those we mostly remember are the stars. We visit Cooperstown and can pass through the section honoring the greatest of the greats—those enshrined in the National Baseball Hall of Fame. Yet those honorees are not the essence of baseball any more than the Rolls-Royce is the essence of automobiles. Baseball honors individual excellence, but it is a team sport. Current major league rosters carry twenty-four players. Few are of star stature. Many are marginal players who will not last four seasons—the minimum number necessary to qualify for a baseball pension.

A big league tenure as a marginal performer must be difficult to endure. Such a player was no doubt a star in high school, in college, or in the minor leagues. Yet in the stratosphere of the big leagues, he is ordinary at best, and will never know the feel of celebrity, of stardom. Some of these players approximated greatness, though, *once* in their otherwise ordinary careers. What must it have been like for such athletes to have a brief taste of what Ted Williams or Sandy Koufax knew throughout their hugely productive careers?

Some of the players profiled in this book had quite credible careers, but only one truly significant season. Willard Marshall, for instance, was named to the National League All-Star team three times. Always an excellent defensive outfielder, he had only one really prodigious year with his bat. The same might be said for former Dodger first baseman Wes Parker—a defensive genius, but a great batter only during the 1970 campaign. Walt Dropo, too, remains fixed in the memories of many fans, doubtless because of his fantastic rookie season. His lifetime statistics are decent, but only in 1950 was he a tremendous all-around hitter.

In researching this book, I identified more than forty players who enjoyed one quality year in the bigs. The stories on the following pages profile eleven who agreed to be interviewed about their "One Shining Season."

Through the process of identifying and locating players profiled in these pages, many people offfered aid, comfort, and suggestions. Among those I would like to thank are my wife, Judy, my tireless first reader; Dave Moore for his constant encouragement; my agent, Jeanne K. Hanson, who believed in this book; Patrick and Yvonne Jones, who graciously extended bed and board while I was in Dallas; and Lloyd Hackl, my American Legion baseball coach in Duluth, Minnesota, who shared with me his love for both baseball and good writing.

INTRODUCTION

by Ira Berkow

This is a mystery book, as much as it is a book of baseball, or old baseball players.

Comes a time in every man's life when he does something right, and not just right, but absolutely, indisputably, gloriously right. Sometimes it occurs in a momentary flash of insight or luck, like finding the direct route within the tangle of lines on a road map. Or it happens in a day, when the leaky roof you patched at home (risking life and limb in the process) actually works this time to keep out the rain.

Or, as described in this intriguing book by Michael Fedo, it can materialize over a full season. At bat, now, the ball no longer seems like a bullet, but a grapefruit—"No," reconsidered Lee Thomas, who had his best slugging season with the Angels in 1962, "like a basketball!"

Or you're on the pitcher's mound and feel supreme confidence, as did Barney Schultz, in his sterling year as a relief pitcher for the 1964 World Champion St. Louis Cardinals. "I remember many nights when I walked in there," said Schultz, "I looked at the hitter and just knew I was gonna strike him out."

For the broadly blessed, for the Ted Williamses and Joe DiMaggios and Bob Gibsons of the world, one great year follows another, or numerous great years are mixed in among the simply superb ones. For others, like those who tell their tales in this book, these less-than-household names—Roger Wolff of the Washington Senators, for example, and Billy Grabarkewitz of the Dodgers and Dave Nicholson of the White Sox, the Orioles, the Astros, and the Braves—there was one stunning season, preceded or followed by either pretty good ones, or mediocre ones, or just plain poor ones.

And for some, as swiftly as they reached a certain height they tumbled from it, like Hurricane Bob Hazle, who batted .403 over the final two months of the pennant-winning season for the 1957 Milwaukee Braves. Sometimes their excellence overlapped from or to other seasons, as it did for Walt Dropo, the Red Sox power hitter, and for Ned Garver, who had a good fourteen-year career but performed the remarkable feat of winning twenty games for a last-place team, the 1951 St. Louis Browns, the first time it had ever been accomplished.

How did these men attain that pinnacle, even ever so briefly? How did they not remain there?

For most, that "home-run groove," as Willard Marshall described it, disappeared. The rhythm that seemed certain to last forever was lost, never to be regained, regardless of how earnestly one sought to plumb the riddle.

Others suffered an injury from which they never would fully recover, physically or psychologically. When Roger Wolff came down with a sore arm during the 1946 season, he was forced by the Senators' hierarchy to continue pitching. This happened in the year following his best season, when he compiled a 20–10 record, the only season in his seven-year career in which he had a better-than-.500 won-loss record. "In those days," said Wolff, "they could take advantage of you"—*they* meaning management. And to this day, he says, "I still can't even rake leaves."

Stan Lopata, meanwhile, was injured when he failed to dodge a fastball at the end of his outstanding season, 1956. He told Fedo: "I got hit in the head and after that . . . I don't know, maybe it was that or maybe I just lost concentration."

Nicholson talked about the constant, burdensome pressure of the media, and Grabarkewitz said that Dixie Walker, the hitting coach of the Dodgers, "over-coached" him. But Wes Parker, in the interview that immediately follows that of his former teammate Grabarkewitz, recalled that the same Dixie Walker saved his career with coaching tips.

Over a cup of coffee in their kitchen, or seated in their living room amid mementoes from their playing days, the onetime ballplayers considered the secrets of success.

Some talked about the need to harness confidence, the need to possess the desire to achieve (even going so far as to become a virtual "recluse" off the ballfield, as Parker said he did during his best season), the need to be understood by a manager or owner (a need which some, like Lee Thomas, when he was with Leo Durocher's Cubs, said wasn't always met); some revealed significant baseball tips, like Grabarkewitz insisting a batter must keep *both* eyes on the ball to be effective, or Parker explaining how he figured out the way to break "the pitcher's code."

With baseball so deeply embedded in the soul of most Americans, and with ballplayers, even old ones (maybe especially old ones), continuing to mean so much to us, it is a particular pleasure to relive with these eleven men their finest moments, however brief.

INTRODUCTION

In *One Shining Season*, gleaned patiently and put down on paper gracefully by Michael Fedo, are the dreams, the memories, the victories and disappointments, and the wisdom of hindsight that most of us in some way can identify with, regardless of whether we ever socked a home run or broke off a dazzling curve, or, for that matter, ever patched a leaky roof.

ONE SHINING SEASON

ROGER WOLFF:

Washington Senators, 1945

"I was sitting by myself in the dining car and Ted [Williams] comes in, and he plops down. 'Goddam,' he said, 'I can't hit you. I can hit Leonard and Niggling, but I can't hit you.'"

To get to Chester, Illinois, you pick up Highway 3 off Interstate 255 and head south. That road follows the Mississippi River all the way to Cairo and the Kentucky border. In Illinois they call it the Great River Route, a supposedly quite scenic drive. But as this two-lane highway winds its way along the river through flat, unadorned countryside, and towns with names that sound New England or Indian—Ellis Groves, New Hanover, Red Bud—the highway, indeed Illinois itself, seems to gaze enviously westward across the expanse of the river at the peaks and bluffs of Missouri, where the landscape holds more eye-pleasing variety. There is a plain ordinariness to these villages, and the years have robbed them of their character, giving them Pizza Huts and replacing Ma and Pa general stores with antiseptic chain operations.

Chester, about sixty miles south of St. Louis, is home to an

Illinois state penitentiary and eight-thousand permanent residents, including Roger Wolff, who brought a measure of fame to the town and all of Randolph County more than forty years ago when he almost pitched the perpetually last-place Washington Senators to an American League pennant. It was in 1945.

Roger Wolff was a sturdy right-handed pitcher then, with a dipsy-doodle knuckleball that baffled most of the league's batters that year. He won twenty games while losing only ten and could have just as easily posted a 24–6 record, because he was on the losing end of four 1–0 games. He finished the year with a 2.12 earned run average.

There are those who would diminish Wolff's accomplishment by pointing out that 1945 was a war year, and many stalwart players were in military service. But the fact that a pitcher didn't have to face perhaps a handful of the game's best batters over the course of a full schedule scarcely detracts from either Wolff's splendid performance or the significant achievements of others who played major league baseball from 1942 to 1945. As the old St. Louis Browns hurler Nelson Potter has said, "You still had to get men out. Batters still had to get base hits, and fielders had to make plays. Some teams lost stars, and the league maybe became more equitable. But that was really the only difference."

The 1945 baseball season remains vivid for Wolff because the Senators were in a tight race, and he won nearly 40 percent of his career victories in that single shining season. Lifetime over seven years in the bigs, he won only fifty-two games while losing sixty-nine. He made his last major league appearance at age thirty-six.

I phone Roger Wolff from a laundromat just inside the city limits upon arriving in Chester. Instead of directing me to his home, he insists on coming to the laundromat and escorting me back to his house. I follow him in his pale blue 1978 Cadillac, which, he proudly informs me, has only forty thousand miles on the odometer.

Roger Wolff is seventy-eight, a widower, and lives alone in a pleasant single-story white house on Knott Street. We sit in his kitchen, where a thin November sun bathes a white wooden table. Wolff is preparing bean soup and coffee on the stove, and though it is barely past ten in the morning, he invites me to join the repast. "Ever' once in a while I get hungry for bean soup with pork." He speaks softly in the semi-Southern dialect native to lower Illinois. His voice is cigarette-laced, a gravelly rattle.

A physically imposing man who earned a reputation as a brawler during his twelve-year minor league career, Wolff has thickened through the middle now and weighs about thirty pounds more than his 205-pound playing weight. He stands a shade over six feet one inch; his thinning hair is gray, framing bifocals. The man is gentle and solicitous; he could be anybody's grandfather. He is not, though, as he and his late wife were childless. He is mildly surprised that I would be interested in interviewing a man who played ball long before I was able to read a box score.

Roger Wolff is my father's age, and in deference to that, I address him as Mr. Wolff. "Call me Roger," he says. "Ever'body else does."

Miles and decades away from the tumult and shouting of that 1945 pennant drive, not decided until the last day of the season, Wolff lives now in quiet retirement in this town he's called home since 1922. That year his father moved the family of six children here to run a grocery store. Wolff still has a lively interest in baseball, but he catches most of it on television. He hasn't stepped inside a major league ballpark in more than fifteen years. "I don't get around much these days," he says. "I've been invited to old-timers' games, but I'm not gonna get out there and make a fool of myself at my age and condition."

Roger is not forgotten by old-time baseball fans, though, and still receives six to ten letters each month requesting autographs. He opens one now and removes a letter and a mint-condition 1945 baseball card with a picture of Roger Wolff at his peak, wearing his Senators uniform and grinning.

Sitting at his kitchen table, fondling the card, Roger Wolff tells me he is proud of his baseball achievements—especially that 1945 season, when he, Dutch Leonard, Johnny Niggling, and Mickey Haefner may have been baseball's only starting rotation whose main pitch was the knuckler.

Wolff has been retired now for nearly thirteen years. In his last job, he served as athletic director at the local state pen, after turns at running a nightclub, selling insurance, and representing a biscuit company.

He pours coffee and lights the first of the dozen cigarettes he'll smoke during the next two hours. "You know, back in '45 we finished up our schedule a couple weeks before the rest of the league, because Griffith Stadium was also used by the Washington Redskins for football. That scheduling made us play a lot of doubleheaders, which hurt us. So we finished the season early. We went out to Bethesda Naval Base and stayed there and worked out there. And then I went with Leonard, Niggling, and the catcher, Rick Ferrell, and Mickey Haefner, I believe, into Detroit to play, if we had to have a playoff game. See, we were there in case the Browns could beat Detroit in a doubleheader on the last day of the season. Then we'd have been tied for first place with the Tigers.

"Potter [the Browns' pitcher] was leading something like three to two in the ninth inning, but, with bases loaded, Greenberg hits one in the stands, and then that's it. If there'd been a playoff game, I'd have pitched it. I'd have got Newhouser, who was a hell of a pitcher. I got him in one of those ball games earlier in the season, which we won three to two. In the first inning I had two men on base, first and second. One out. Batter hit a ground ball to shortstop. He went to Fred Vaughn—out at second, to first for a double play. But the runner at second was safe, because Vaughn juggled the ball." He grimaces slightly as he recounts the incident. He sighs and continues.

"I had men at second and third with two outs. But Cullenbine punched a knuckleball over short for a Texas leaguer, and two runs scored. And I said to myself, that's all they can have—they can't have any more. We went ahead three to two. And in the eighth inning, the first two men singled off me. They were sacrificed over to second and third. Then Doc Cramer comes up, a left-handed hitter. Rudy York is up next, and he's a right-handed hitter. Rick Ferrell says, 'Put him on, Rog.' But I don't want to. He walks out and says, 'Would you rather pitch to Cramer?' I says, 'Yeah, but I'm not the boss. If the boss says put him on, that's what I haveta do.'"

The vivid richness of Roger's recall amazes me. I would have guessed that to a ballplayer, games might have blended one into another, and it would take a perusal of scrapbooks to prod the memory, to really remember how it was, unless, of course, the game took on extraordinary dimensions, such as a no-hitter or grand slam home run. But Roger is on a roll, rocking back in his chair, a faint smile playing over his lips. He clears his throat and goes on.

"So Ossie Bluege, our manager, comes running out from the bench. He says, 'You rather pitch to Cramer?' I says, 'Yeah.' He says, 'Well, make him hit a knuckleball.' I says, 'Don't you worry about that. That's all he's gonna see.' But I didn't want to put him on, and then maybe get behind York and have to come in to him. So I had two men to pitch to. I wasn't going to walk Cramer intentionally. And I did get him, and we won the game.

"But we lost the pennant, and I still wonder how many times Bluege thought about this. Boston had a pitcher named Boo Ferris. He was pitching against us and we scored five runs off him the first inning. Marino Pieretti's pitching for us, a little right-hander. In the sixth innning I said to Bluege, 'The kid's bouncing them up there. He doesn't have his stuff anymore. Let me go in there and save this game for you.' He said, 'Roger, you gotta go out and pitch Sunday's game.' I said, 'I can pitch two-three innings and still pitch Sunday.' This is Friday night. Well, I'll be damned, instead of him going out there—and it's now five to three—he calls time. Instead of stalling for a little more time, he's gonna make a change. So I run down to the bullpen. Alex Carrasquel was down there too, but Bluege doesn't call me. He goes to Carrasquel and Bob Johnson tripled off him and tied the game. Then Bluege brings me in and I went until the sixteenth inning and they got a run off me and I lost the game. But we had it there. And I lost my turn on Sunday too. All he had to do was walk out there and take a little time. I was about ready anyway. This was late in the season on our last road trip. If I get Johnson we win, and we're tied with Detroit."

It is a situation Roger Wolff has obviously relived endlessly over the years, and he dwells on what might have been. He mentions his relatively brief big league tenure now too, maintaining that all things being equal, he could have continued pitching until the age of forty-three or forty-four. "To be honest with you, with that knuckleball I had I think I could have played until I was fifty."

That knuckleball he'd perfected was born in Chester, he tells me, where young Roger would pitch to his brother alongside the family store during breaks and after work. "The mayor of our town came by one day and he said, 'Let me show you how to throw a ball that does things.' So he showed me how to throw the knuckleball. I threw it like he did, with three fingers, not two. And I never gripped the seams or the ball would spin on me. I picked it up right away. I just loved baseball. I used to get on my bicycle and go to the field, and I'd stay out there until you couldn't see the ball anymore." The old knuckleballer reaches for his coffee, which he has not yet touched. It has grown cold. He does not pour himself a fresh cup. Instead he dumps the contents of his cup into a small pan and starts warming it on his electric stove.

The old Chester ballfield where Roger learned his craft is gone now, covered by condos at the south end of town. There's a neat new facility on Highway 3 at the north approach, but, says Wolff, the atmosphere isn't the same. There's no town team now, and the Bud Cohen Field is mainly used by Little Leaguers.

Wolff got his first taste of play for pay pitching for Red Bud, the town twenty miles up Highway 3, in the semipro St. Moran League, during the early thirties. He got $25 per game—"big money for a kid during the Depression," he recalled. "Yessir, I couldn't make that in a week at the store." He pours his reheated coffee back into his cup, then fills mine with fresh from the pot. He sits at the table again, ignoring his coffee, fondling his cigarette lighter.

"You know, even in the big leagues, I never warmed up but the catcher wouldn't put on his mask. I mean, I had something on that ball. Lots of times I'd have to put my glove in front of my face to keep from laughing at the batter trying to hit that thing.

"I just knew I was a good pitcher. I didn't think anybody could hit me. I remember—this was before I come up with Philadelphia in '41—that I wished I could have pitched to DiMaggio when he had that big fifty—fifty-six-game streak going. I tell you, he'd have seen nothing but knuckleballs.

"A batter had to beat me on my pitch. Or else, by God, I may walk him. And I absolutely say, if a catcher can't catch it, how in hell can a hitter hit it? I'm not kidding you. Shoot. I had a pretty good catcher in Ferrell, but we had another catcher, a guy from Cuba, Mike Guerra. He could catch that knuckleball better than those other guys. One day when we were in Chicago, Bluege comes to me and asks who I want to catch me. 'Rick just can't catch every day and catch you too,' he says. 'You're just too hard to catch.' 'Well,' I said, 'Guerra can catch the knuckleball better than about anybody.' See, I wasn't fast—I had only a mediocre fastball—but it's hard to find a man who can catch that knuckleball."

Wolff reflects, in the quiet of his kitchen, that he capped his career season by pitching a 2–0 shutout against Philadelphia for his twentieth win. He also pitched a one-hitter that year against the Athletics, facing only twenty-eight batters. Hal Peck's fourth-inning single ruined Roger's bid for baseball immortality. "I never thought about a no-hitter, I just wanted to win. And wouldn't you know but Peck was my roommate when we were at Cleveland together in 1947. He comes up to me and says, 'Damn, Roger, I sure wish I'da never got that base hit off you.' 'Well, hell,' I says, 'don't think that. That's baseball.'" He chuckles, and repeats, "That's baseball."

Wolff won consistently in 1945, and the Senators finished with an 87–67 record. Along with Wolff's twenty wins, Leonard won seventeen, and Mickey Haefner won sixteen games. "The fellas made plays behind me," Wolff recalled, "and that old knuckleball, I'm telling you, just jumped all over. See, I had a lot of confidence, and then when I pitched, the boys had confidence in me that I was going to win the game. By God, I did too, didn't I?"

Wolff has less pleasant memories of 1944, the year before his great season, when he suffered through his worst major league season, winning only four games while losing fifteen. His earned run average soared to nearly five. He had been traded by the Athletics to Washington after a credible 10–15 season. The trade stemmed from Wolff's dissatisfaction over not receiving a $300 bonus from Connie Mack in 1943.

"I'll tell you, you don't stand a chance with those last-place teams up there," Wolff said, lighting another cigarette. "I had a bonus contract that if we drew four hundred thousand people I would get three hundred dollars. But this was just a verbal agreement; it wasn't written down.

"I came in the clubhouse the day before the last game of the year and bumped into our first baseman, Dick Siebert, who had the same contract I did. He said, 'Roger, why don't you go see Mr. Mack? I got my bonus. But don't give me away, though.'

"So I went on up and I said, 'Mr. Mack, I've come about my bonus.' 'Well,' he said, 'we didn't hit four hundred thousand, Roger.' We were something over three hundred and seventy thousand. Just imagine teams drawing that today. So I said, 'Well, I thought you might give me part of it.' He wouldn't give it to me, so I asked him to trade me. He said, 'You really feel that way?' I said, 'I sure do.'"

Actually Wolff pitched decently for the A's in '42 and '43, but was hampered by the quality of the team playing behind him. Those teams finished last each year, winning only fifty-five and forty-nine games respectively. Wolff was responsible for twelve wins in '43 and ten in '44.

"Anyway," he continues, "I ended up with Washington. And I had a miserable year in 1944."

I ask him what happened in 1944: did he lose control of his best pitch?

"I had constant pain in my left shoulder," he says. "I couldn't sleep. I had to sleep sitting in a chair. I thought I had a broken vertebra, and I went to the hospital and they told me to see my dentist. I told 'em I always went to the dentist twice a year. But the doc, he said, 'Go see your dentist.'

"I went to the dentist, and I had ten abscessed teeth. I got those out and went and took these baths and I felt the pain just go on out of my arm." He runs his right hand down the length of his left arm.

"Now in Washington, my wife and I rented Griff's [club owner Clark Griffith's] daughter's apartment. Joe Haynes, a pitcher with Chicago, married her. When they'd leave Washington, I had their apartment. So Griff came to me and said, 'I don't think Thelma is going out this year. Look for an apartment someplace else.'

"Well, we opened the season and I beat the Yankees two

straight. Both times two to one. So Griff says, 'Say, Thelma is gonna go out to Chicago with Joe after all. So if you still want that apartment, it's yours.' See, he didn't think I was gonna be there long."

I have read an old *Washington Post* story that was making the rounds early in the 1945 season, when Wolff's stats were appearing among the ranks of league-leading pitchers. According to the story, after the 1944 season finale in Washington, the dejected Wolff was on his way to his car outside Griffith Stadium when a young teenage boy asked Wolff to teach him to throw a slider. I mention the story and Wolff says he recalls that while he never refused a request for an autograph, he wasn't in the mood to take time with the kid. But he agreed anyway.

"Old George Uhle taught me that pitch, while he was coach of the pitchers, but I never much used it," Wolff said. However, after fooling around with the slider that afternoon, Wolff brought it to spring training with him in 1945, and added another reliable pitch to his arsenal. "Of course, the knuckleball was still my bread-and-butter pitch, and I'll tell you what. I had a ball game against Lefty Lee of the White Sox, and we were tied nothin' to nothin' in the eighth, and I struck out the hitter and the catcher dropped the ball when there were two outs. But the man on third scored and they had a one-to-nothing lead. Rick Ferrell said, 'Goddam, Rog, it looks like I lost this game for you.' I said, 'No, we got our bats in the last half of the eighth and the ninth. We'll get something going.' We scored three runs in the bottom of the eighth and won it. That's how the year went. We seemed to find ways to win ball games. And I was just sure nobody could hit me when I pitched.

"You understand, I couldn't throw all knuckleballs because I would tear my finger." He looks for a long moment at the tip of the middle finger on his right hand. He is drifting back over time, feeling again the pain of blisters or ripped skin. He grimaces slightly. "So anyway, I got this slider down—nothing more than a nickel curve really—and it gave me a little something extra."

That extra pitch, he now thinks, may have turned the corner for him in 1945. An article in a Washington newspaper about midseason in '45 mentioned that Wolff had been one of the Senators' worst pitchers in '44, and less than a year later had become the team's ace. The piece also said that after '44, Clark Griffith tried to trade Roger, but no other American League team was interested in his services. There was lots of interest in him at the conclusion of 1945, but Griffith had no intention of trading Wolff then. Indeed, he rewarded Roger with his best-ever major league salary—$14,000 for 1946.

It was hard-earned money in those days, and Clark Griffith was never loose with the purse strings. Looking back on that season, Roger Wolff lays blame for it, and the subsequent demise of his career, on the parsimonious Griffith.

Though he ended with a 5–8 won-loss record, Wolff still achieved a highly credible ERA of 2.58.

He snuffs a cigarette in a glass ashtray and clears his throat. "I was finished on July the fourth, 1946. I was pitching against the Yankees. Joe Kuhel was playing first base and Cecil Travis was playing shortstop. One out, and a ground ball was hit in the hole by first. Kuhel makes a good throw to Travis, and I go over to make the play at first. The throw from Travis was a bit behind me and I twisted to catch the ball." He is standing now, demonstrating how he leaned backward to receive the toss. "I trip over the bag and tear a muscle in my back. We didn't have disabled lists back then. They sent me to Griffith's personal doctor and he told me not to throw.

"A few days later Griff came to me and said, 'I want you to cut loose.' I told him I couldn't; the doc said no throwing.

"Griff insisted, and told me to tell that to Dr. Larkin when I went for my treatment the next day. Doc, he was just as insistent, and he gave me a letter to show Mr. Griffith. The letter repeated, absolutely no throwing. I gave it to Griff and he says, 'Bah.' Then he called downstairs to a secretary and said, 'Make a reservation for Wolff to leave on a sleeper tonight and join the club in Cleveland.' Roger's creased face darkens into a frown. He exhales slowly, a deep sigh.

"I went into the hotel coffee shop next morning for breakfast and Bluege comes in and sits down. 'How you feeling, Roger?' he says. 'Terrible,' I told him. 'I don't know what I'm doing here. Doctor said I shouldn't be here.' 'Well,' he says, 'what're you gonna do?'

"I told him I always trusted the Cardinals' doctor, Dr. Highland, and when we got to St. Louis I was gonna see him, and if he said the same thing as Dr. Larkin, I was gonna tell Griffith to stick it up his can. I was gonna do what the doctor said."

But Roger Wolff played baseball in an era when athletes were not pampered. They played with pain because that's what was expected. Complaints of nagging injuries were rare, and players kept quiet, often to the detriment of their careers.

"All the same, you see, I wanted to be eligible for a pension, and you had to get five years in to be eligible. I was never one to dodge pitching. I mean, gimme that ball, and I'll pitch.

"But Bluege must have called Griffith back, and he pitched me batting practice that night. I'm telling you, and I'm not exaggerating, I couldn't hardly get myself out of bed the next morning. So when I got to the clubhouse, Bluege asked me how I felt, and I said, 'Ossie, I just feel terrible.'

"We went right on to St. Louis and I went to Dr. Highland and he told me, 'Roger, don't even dress. You may unconsciously pick up a ball, and you can't do it. No throwing whatsoever for the rest of the season.' This was a real serious muscle tear.

"Well, they pitched me the next day and I hurt it worse. I was traded the next year to Cleveland. And I couldn't get anybody out. I just couldn't, it hurt so damn bad. So I was traded to Pittsburgh, and after the 1947 season I went to Dr. Highland in

St. Louis and he told me I'd better hang up my glove. He told me, 'If you hurt it again, it'll probably be permanent.' But you know something? I still can't even rake leaves." Roger Wolff gingerly runs his fingers over the forty-two-year-old injury and shakes his head.

"See, most guys like Griffith and Connie Mack hate to pay a guy that money if he isn't playing. Here I thought I was gonna pitch until I was forty-three or forty-four."

Arriving in the big leagues at all was something of a struggle for Wolff, as it was for most major leaguers of his generation. There were only sixteen teams total in both leagues then, so earning a position on a big league roster was enormously competitive. Many ballplayers were career minor leaguers, some toiling upward of twenty years without ever receiving so much as an invitation to major league spring training. Others, having gotten an opportunity, performed commendably, even hit .300, but sometimes lasted only one or two seasons. They may have alienated a manager or the owner, or even a valuable veteran player, and so they were returned to the minors. Other talented players were restricted by their minor league contracts. An owner of a minor league franchise in the thirties or forties, recognizing a meal-ticket performer, sometimes refused to sell that player to a higher classification. Wolff himself was victimized by this system.

He was up and down in the middle-minor leagues, starting with Danville in 1930, he said, then on to Terre Haute, Indianapolis, Fort Worth, and Dayton, Ohio, where he pitched nearly four seasons. After the Three-I League blew up in 1932, as revenues fell short of operating expenses, Wolff, who had been the property of the St. Louis Cardinals, was signed by the Dodgers. "They wanted to assign me to York in the Pennsylvania League," he recalled. "Frank Dessau managed there, and I played for him in Decatur, Illinois, in 1932. And oh my God, he'd second-guess you. He'd say, 'What'd that fella hit off you? Curveball? Knuckleball? What'd you throw him that for?'

"So he was managing now at York, and I told Max Carey, who was managing the Dodgers at the time, and who, by the way, was a very religious man, that I wouldn't play for that sonofabitch Dessau for nothing. Max says, 'That's a bad name to call anybody.' 'I know it,' I says, 'but in my book that's what he is.'

"Anyway, I said they could send me to Dayton, under Ducky Holmes. I liked Ducky, he treated me swell, and I won for him too—seventeen-eighteen games a year. So in 1936 when I went to training with them, the clubhouse boy comes down with a paper from the last winter that says I was supposed to be sold to Atlanta. Well, I went to see Holmes, and I said, 'I see you could have sold me.'

"'Yeah, I could have sold you,' he says. So I told him, 'What the hell's the matter? I don't want to be stuck here if I can go up to Atlanta. My ambition is to get up the ladder.' He said, 'Roger, you ask twenty or thirty thousand dollars for a man like you, they almost fall off their chair.' This is back in the thirties when things were rough.

"He tells me to stick with him one more year and he'd sell me the next. I really had no choice, because I'd already signed my contract. Then he sold me to Davenport in the Western League. And then I started moving along. Oklahoma City in the Texas League was next."

Wolff pitched for fourteen minor league teams in seven different leagues during his struggle to make the major leagues. And he thinks a lot of what he sees in big league baseball today would pass for decent minor league play forty to fifty years ago. "If a guy made the majors by the time he was twenty-five, twenty-six years old, he was doing fine," Wolff says. "A fella learned to play in the minor leagues. You make a mistake and your manager would say, 'You were supposed to learn how to do that in the minor leagues.' Now, you got these kids nineteen, twenty years old playing in the big leagues, and they're still learning.

"Back then, though, I'll tell you, they could take advantage of you. You signed your contract, and it was take it or leave it. The salaries these fellas get today, why . . ." His voice trails off. "But I'll tell you something, boy. I had me some knuckleball." He gazes out the window, the look in his eye distant, faraway. He is drifting, on this November day, back to September of 1941, and he has just been called up by the Philadelphia Athletics. "My first game in the big leagues I pitched against Dutch Leonard in Washington, and lost a two-hitter one to nothing. Then one time Ted Williams said I was the toughest pitcher for him to hit up there. I beat them one day in Boston seven to two, and they were going into New York and we were heading back to Philadelphia on the same train. I was sitting by myself in the dining car and Ted comes in, and he plops down. 'Goddam,' he said, 'I can't hit you. I can hit Leonard and Niggling, but I can't hit you.'

"I had very good luck with him. I had some knuckleball. I had a game one day in Philadelphia in '42 and Williams was the hitter, and there's a man on first. I threw him three straight knuckleballs and he swung at all three and missed them. But the catcher missed every one of them too. The runner went to second, then third, and scored. Frankie Hayes was catching then, but he never caught me one ball."

Wolff pours more coffee, lights another cigarette, and chuckles softly. "There were times when I done a little cheating." He pantomimes delivering a pitch and following through. As he completes the motion, he licks his fingers. 'I wet a few every now and then, and would signal my catcher every time the ball was loaded. You make your pitch," he says, pantomiming again, "and while the ball is traveling you wet your fingers. 'Cause everybody is watching the ball, and unless you know somebody's watching you, you could get away with it. Old Cal Hubbard came out to me one day and he says, 'Damn, I been umpiring up here a long time and I never saw a better spitter than that.'" He chuckles again. "'Course, I didn't have to throw one often, but I'd use it to cross up a hitter."

The sun leaves the kitchen and it's time for me to depart. Roger Wolff puts out his cigarette. "I really believe, ever'thing considered, that I had a real successful career and life." He shows me several more photos of his late wife. "This little girl really kept me going," he says. "Kept me from running around and raising all kinds of hell. Yeah, she was something."

At the door I shake hands with him but sense he hasn't quite finished talking. "Drive careful now," he cautions. There's a brief pause, then he speaks again, quietly but with urgency. "I really thought I'd play this game until I was fifty." He smacks his right fist into his left palm—a kid pounding his glove. "I did. I had me some knuckleball."

ROGER WOLFF'S MAJOR LEAGUE CAREER

Year	Team	Games	Won	Lost	ERA
1941	Athletics	2	0	2	3.19
1942	Athletics	32	12	15	3.32
1943	Athletics	41	10	15	3.54
1944	Senators	33	4	15	4.99
1945	Senators	33	20	10	2.12
1946	Senators	21	5	8	2.58
1947	Indians	7	0	0	3.94
1947	Pirates	13	1	4	8.70
TOTALS		**182**	**52**	**69**	**3.41**

WILLARD MARSHALL:

New York Giants, 1947

"That was another thing that frustrated me. When I came up in 1942, I was a dead pull hitter. Always a pull hitter. Then all of a sudden, I lost the ability to pull."

Fort Lee, New Jersey, is the last exit off the Jersey Turnpike before the George Washington Bridge disgorges the traveler into the bowels of New York. It is a small, crowded suburb with narrow one-way streets which meld and converge in a mystifying fashion, so that it's possible to drive around the block, as I did on its downtown streets, and not come out in the place from which you started. No doubt sensing this when I phoned him the night before from Princeton, former All-Star New York Giants outfielder Willard Marshall told me not to bother getting directions to his home because I'd no doubt become confused in the traffic, which he called "a pain in the ass." Instead, he directed me to the Fort Lee Café, and said he'd meet me there and take me to his home.

When I finally locate the restaurant, he is standing outside, a tall, handsome man, looking much younger than his sixty-eight years, a man with ramrod-straight posture and a full head of dark, wavy hair. Though the day is cloudy and damp, he seems comfortable in a long-sleeved golf shirt and appears not to need a coat or jacket. I follow him in his car to a fashionable neighborhood on Arcadian Way, and we pull into the driveway of his spacious home, situated among other large, well-appointed houses that have been constructed on a cliff that drops down to the Hudson River. The view of Manhattan across the river from Willard and Marie Marshall's backyard walk-out is nothing less than spectacular.

Willard Marshall escorts me into his living room, where a framed photograph of him in his 1942 Giants uniform hangs above the fireplace. The portrait is flanked by a pair of bronzed baseball shoes on one side and a bronzed Giants cap on the other. On the coffee table before us is a miniature of the Greek sculpture *The Wrestlers.*

Marshall has held a variety of jobs since leaving baseball after the 1955 season, most notably running an insurance and real estate business with his father-in-law. At the time of our interview, on an early afternoon in late January, he has been officially retired for four months, "though my wife thinks I should go back to work," he says with a laugh. "But I'm not tired of my inactivity yet. I play golf, visit friends," who include former major leaguers who reside in the area, Tommy Holmes, his old teammate from the Braves, and former Yankee first baseman Joe Collins, who passed away after our interview.

Before we settle down, he walks to a large bookcase and removes a slim volume of poetry published by one of his daughters, D. L. Marshall. "Bein' you're a writer," he says, handing me the book, "I thought you might be interested in this." He smiles, obviously proud of his daughter's accomplishment.

Finally, we head back to the conversation area of the room, where a sofa and several chairs are in a horseshoe arrangement.

"Who else are you seeing for this book?" he asks in a soft Virginia dialect, as I unpack my recorder and notebooks. I mention a few names, and he nods in recognition.

He is softspoken, courtly, inquiring if I'd like tea or coffee, and pointing out the location of the downstairs bathroom, should I need it.

Willard Marshall played eleven seasons in the major leagues, and throughout his career he was noted for his solid defensive play. Always a strong thrower, he twice led National League outfielders in assists. No fluke with the bat either, Marshall achieved a creditable lifetime batting average of .274. However, in 1947, he discovered a long-ball stroke, along with many of the rest of the Giants, who hit a league record 221 homers. Johnny Mize led the team and the league that year with fifty-one, but Marshall powered thirty-six himself, drove in 107 runs, and batted .291. 1947 was the only year in his big league tenure he hit more than seventeen home runs.

He is amused to learn that when I was a young boy I owned a baseball All-Star board game, and he was a prominent performer. I recall a rather large band on his card for home runs, so it must have been a collection of the 1947 All-Star teams.

"Must have been," he agrees.

Since he hit so many homers in '47, I ask him to tell me what he thinks happened that year.

"I have no idea," he says. "I always believed I had the power, but just never produced that many home runs again. I have no idea why. I guess I was just swinging in the right spots. I don't think there was any reason for it, though I never had another year like that. What can you say? There were guys that year who hit home runs who'd never hit them before, for some reason. Who knows? It was just one of those years. Guys like Rigney, Blattner, Buddy Kerr would hit twelve, thirteen, seventeen home runs. It was just a year when it seemed like everybody was hittin' them."

I asked if he thought the incredibly short 252-foot right-field porch in the Polo Grounds perhaps influenced him to reach the seats that year.

He shakes his head. "Not really. The Polo Grounds had that short right field and short left field, but you had to be a real good pull hitter to get those. You know, center field was tremendous. Very few balls were hit out there. In fact, only two or three got in those center-field bleachers in the whole history of the Polo Grounds. Yeah, that was a big center field."

The biggest day in Marshall's career also occurred in his magnificent 1947 season. On July 17, in a game against the Cincinnati Reds, Marshall clubbed home runs in three consecutive trips to the plate. I ask him what he remembers about that day, expecting a lengthy anecdote rich with details and description.

Instead my question is followed by a long pause as he reflects. "You know, I can't remember who I even hit 'em off of." He pauses again. "But naturally anytime you hit three home runs you're very proud of the feat. But I don't remember who I hit them off of. I think maybe one of them was a guy named Ray Scarborough. It was against Cincinnati, I remember that, but can't recall who was pitching."

Hoping to jog his memory, I ask if he recalls the circumstances, such as how many men were on base, or in what innings he hit the homers.

He offers an apologetic smile. "No, I really don't. I know some guys can remember almost everything. I've talked to guys who can tell you every ball they ever hit. But somebody asks me— whoooooo—I really have to think. I'd really have to concentrate on that, I guess. Now, I remember playing in that no-hitter Rex Barney [of the Dodgers] pitched against us. And there are certain other things."

Would one of them, I ask, be his amazing steal of home

against Warren Spahn? This theft really was astounding, because Marshall, noted as a slow runner, was the lead man in an incredible triple steal. Behind him were Johnny Mize and Walker Cooper, the other two Giants in the triumvirate manager Leo Durocher called "the thundering herd." But here too, his recollection of his only career theft of home is fuzzy.

"I wasn't fast enough to steal many bases," he says. In fact, he is credited with only fourteen steals in his eleven years in the big leagues. "But I guess I don't really consider that I really stole home. It seemed to me like it was a dropped ball by the catcher, but I don't remember if there was a signal on to steal home or what. Unless I just looked at Spahn and thought he was kickin' his leg too high in the air, and somehow I thought I was gonna make it." He smiles now, also amazed at the feat. "A triple steal. Now that was an accomplishment. To steal against Spahn was something. Why we did it, though, I can't answer. All I know is that Mize and Cooper and I sure couldn't steal many bases." He chuckles.

I have hoped that he'd be able to flesh out responses to my questions, to bring alive details, incidences. So far, he doesn't seem able to do this, though he is not guarding his privacy. In fact, he tells me that his address as listed in the *Baseball Address List* is incorrect, and he is going to send the correct address to the publisher. This is not the action of a former major leaguer who wants to be left alone. The *Baseball Address List* exists solely for autograph collectors who wish to contact current and former players and have baseball cards and other memorabilia signed. Several other ex-players I've talked to say they resent autograph requests, and some former stars—household names— routinely return such requests unopened. Marshall, however, says he still enjoys the recognition, says fans put players on a pedestal and deserve to be treated with courtesy. He would never, he insists, refuse an autograph request.

I redirect the conversation back to 1947 and ask if he thought he was establishing standards for himself that year that would become the norm for him during the remainder of his big league tenure.

"Sure. I always thought I was capable of hitting like that. Yeah. It never happened, but I still think about it. A fella who's able to hit the ball any distance should be able to hit a lot of home runs. Twenty or thirty. Of course, there never have been many who could consistently do that."

I wonder then if his power seemed concentrated into the alleys rather than straight down the line, where fences are more reachable.

He nods vigorously and sits forward, animated now for the first time. "That was another thing that frustrated me. When I came up in 1942, I was a dead pull hitter. Always a pull hitter. Then all of a sudden, I lost the ability to pull." He smiles, then laughs. "I guess maybe the pitchers had something to do with that."

The following season, 1948, Marshall managed only fourteen home runs along with a .272 batting average. And his loss of home run power was duly noted by Durocher and the other coaches who tried to help him regain what he'd apparently lost. The result was, Marshall now thinks, that he may have been overcoached.

"Teaching anybody how to hit is a fallacy," he states emphatically. "I don't believe you can teach anybody to hit. The guy who's goin' to hit has a good eye and quick reaction. Now, you might help him by changin' his feet position or whatever. But when he swings the bat he's got his own rhythm, his own reaction. I've seen Mize and them guys teach." He shakes his head. "Now Westrum," he says, referring to the old stalwart defensive catcher, Wes, "look at Westrum. How many people worked with him? They tried to teach him how to hit. He was a hell of a catcher, but couldn't hit. And I don't think you can teach a guy how to hit."

Marshall is leaning forward now, his voice crackling with enthusiasm. He has traversed the decades and it is 1947 or 1948 again. He touches his arm. "I always had a good arm—I mean I could throw." He pantomimes releasing the ball. "I always figured, and I always taught the young guys I worked with, that you couldn't be afraid of charging the ball. I know a lot of outfielders who had as good an arm or better than I did. But they never threw anybody out. They played too deep and would wait upon a ground ball to get to them. Billy Southworth [a longtime manager in the National League] up in Boston one time said to me that he liked the way I played outfield because I fielded the ball just like a third baseman. I just kept coming in on it and came up throwing. And I used to try to teach the kids that. Trouble with most kids is they get near the ball and they stop. They're afraid they're gonna make an error. Once you stop you can't throw anybody out. You throw a guy out by a step ninety-nine percent of the time. Once you stop and then get ready to throw the ball, it's too late. One of my best friends was Sid Gordon, and I used to talk to him. 'What do you play so deep for? You got a great arm.' And he did. But he very seldom threw anybody out. He was a good ballplayer, a good hitter. In those days they'd compare Carl Furillo and myself with throwing out guys. Furillo. I think he may have had a little stronger arm than I did, but I was pretty accurate. Wasn't too often I missed the cutoff man." He smiles and chuckles again.

He tells me that he loved playing in New York, but doesn't hold it against Leo Durocher for trading him to Boston after the 1949 season, in a trade that brought Alvin Dark and Eddie Stanky to the Giants. "No, I always thought he was a good manager. Durocher didn't care for me for the same reason he didn't care for Mize or Cooper or Gordon. He wanted a running ball club. I don't think Durocher had anything against me, except I just wasn't his type of ballplayer. When he traded Kerr and myself and Sid Gordon to Boston and got Stanky and Dark, that's when he made his ball club."

While the Dark-Stanky-led Giants were beginning to move up the ladder, and would produce that dramatic 1951 pennant playoff win over the Dodgers, Marshall's career went into decline after 1949. In 1950 he batted only .235, hit five homers, and drove in forty runs. When I ask him what happened in 1950, he says with laconic indifference, "I was just starting to go the other way, I guess. I didn't have many decent years after that." He was through as a player in 1955, finishing with the White Sox, after two seasons with Cincinnati.

Marshall's professional baseball career began in 1940 when he was a student at Wake Forest. Just before ending his sophomore year at college, he signed a contract with Atlanta in the Southern Association and played there two years. "Right after the war broke out, the Dodgers had first call on me from Atlanta. And they were gonna take me with them," he said. "But they backed away, and the Giants said they would take me as far as spring training the next year. So that was a lucky break for me."

Bill Terry signed Marshall for New York, offering him a $7,500 bonus. "Now that was a lot of money in those days," he says, nodding. "It sure was. And you know, the best thing baseball did for me was to get me off the farm in Virginia. That was a tough life. And with what I made playing ball, I had a nice living.

"So anyway I had a real good spring in '42 with the Giants and they brought me north." He responded well as a rookie, and was named to the National League All-Star team, mainly because of his defensive play. At the plate he batted .257, with eleven homers and fifty-nine RBI. He would spend the next three seasons in military service.

Surprisingly, he had no difficulty getting back in the baseball groove after serving in the Marines. "I'd played some ball in the service, so I wasn't tremendously out of shape when I got discharged in April of '46. The Giants were coming north from

Florida, traveling by train. I was at my folks' in Richmond, and they were playing an exhibition game in Richmond, before the start of the season. I joined them in Richmond without having any spring training and was in the lineup opening day."

He was still young then, only twenty-five, and though Mel Ott's team finished last in the National League, Marshall hit a steady .282, with thirteen home runs and forty-eight RBI—solid numbers, but certainly no foretokening of his power explosion in 1947.

As he reflects again on 1947, a thought comes to him. "Now I had a real good year in '47, and another thing was I could always hit Ewell Blackwell." He chuckles. "He was my 'cousin'. I hit him very well, and he was a tough pitcher, as you probably remember. But I could always hit Blackwell, for some reason.

"You may remember that he had a streak going where he'd won sixteen games in a row. Well, we beat him—the Giants beat him when he was going for that seventeenth straight win. I hit a home run that tied up the game. And Buddy Kerr got a base hit to drive in the winning run. I forget what inning it was. But anyway . . ." He leans forward and laughs. "I saw Blackwell a couple years ago and he said, 'If I could have gotten you and Bama Howell out, I could have had a hell of a career.'" He laughs again. "We could hit him. But really there wasn't anybody I was *happy* to hit against. Carl Erskine of the Dodgers was the toughest right-hander for me. Warran Spahn was always tough. They had a relief pitcher with the St. Louis Cardinals that most people never heard of, Alpha Brazle. Earl Torgerson and I always hated him. He was tough. We couldn't hit him with a two-by-four. But the Cardinals had a lot of good left-handers in those days. Howie Pollet and Harry Brecheen were tough to hit against."

A left-handed batter, Marshall, as might be expected, had more difficulty hitting against left-handed pitchers. However, he said, "They never took your bat out of the lineup like they do now. You played against everybody. And you might have a bad day, but the next day you got a couple base hits and things evened out. I mean, what do pinch hitters hit today—.200? You have to be in the lineup every day if you're gonna hit. Today there are good ballplayers hitting .230, because they only play half of the season. Every time a left-handed pitcher comes out, they put up a right-handed hitter, and vice versa. How you gonna hit for any average when you don't play? Casey Stengel started all this platooning business in '50 or '51."

The old outfielder waves his hand in disgust. He was glad to play in an era when a man who earned a spot as a regular was expected to play every day, and to play even when in great physical stress. "You knew the job was yours, and you'd have to mess up to lose it. If you were a reserve you had to hope somebody got hurt bad before you could play. They had to carry the regulars off. Except the relief pitchers on the Giants in those days." He laughs heartily. "They got a lot of work." He laughs again. "Our starting pitchers outside of Larry Jansen didn't last too long.

"I was very fortunate in that I never had anything major happen." He chuckles again. "Of course, I couldn't run fast enough to do anything to my legs. If you were playing for Durocher you had to be hurt pretty good or he wouldn't believe you. But that's the way Ott and most of the managers were back in those days. If you were hurt, you'd come out early and get taped up and play. Back then they thought heat was everything. Which was wrong. They've proved that was wrong. But even in those days when I was playing, you pulled a muscle and you got put in hot water. They'd push on you and tape you up. Now when you get hurt, they put you right on ice. And you gotta stay off it until it heals. I remember Ott playing with both legs taped so tight with a pulled muscle he could hardly walk. How he ever got well, I don't know. But that's how we played."

His wife, Marie, enters the room. A pleasant, vivacious woman plagued by recent health problems, she has difficulty getting around. She insists on fending for herself, however, and sits in a wing-back chair. She says she and Willard have been married forty-one years, and that she had never seen a game until she met him. "I love it here," she says. "We live right next door to where I grew up."

She wonders if I have asked Willard about the day he hit three home runs. I tell her I have, but that he doesn't remember it very well. Perhaps she recalls the occasion more vividly than he.

"Oh no," she says. "I didn't know Willard then. But I remember those three home runs because of a money clip he has that an actress gave him—a sort of commemoration of it."

Willard rises, asks his wife and me if he can get us soft drinks or beer. I take a ginger ale, and before I can proceed with questions, he resumes talking.

Still standing before his chair, casting a solicitous glance at Marie, he says, "I hit my first home run in the second ball game I ever played in. Maybe it was the third. But I hit my first home run off Kirby Higbe. I hit it to right field. I hit my last one with the White Sox, but can't remember the guy I hit that off of." He sits.

Carl Hubbell and Bill Terry, two New York Giants legends, have recently passed away, and as we are chatting, Marshall mentions them, and says he played with Hubbell in 1942. He retreats to another room and returns with a large photo of the 1942 team, and points to Hubbell, then begins naming other players pictured. Finally he leans the photo against the coffee table and takes his place on the sofa.

"I played under some good managers in my career," he says, reflecting. "I also played for Rogers Hornsby in Cincinnati. He was not likable. There was nothing to like about him. He hated it when guys laughed or had fun. He didn't think life should be anything but baseball. Once we were up there at Cooperstown to play ball in the Hall of Fame game. And on the bus Andy

Seminick and a pitcher, Frank Smith, were singing 'The old gray mare, she ain't what she used to be,' and carrying on. Hornsby's face kept getting redder and redder, and he called them in when we got back and fined both of them two hundred dollars. Then Smith told Hornsby, 'Gee, I didn't think we were that good.'" He laughs, enjoying the anecdote.

Finally I ask him what he did after the White Sox released him about midseason in 1955.

"When I stopped playing, I went down to Waterloo and managed for the White Sox for the balance of that year. The next year I was a scout. They'd wanted me to stay in Waterloo and manage for another year, but I didn't want to. I just packed it in and came home. I scouted for the Giants a couple years, and then went into real estate with my father-in-law. But I didn't like to scout. So I went to work for a living." He smiles. "Then I got involved with the town of Fort Lee as a recreation director. Between all the things I made a little money.

"But I loved baseball. I did. And if I'm proud of anything in my career it would have to be for never getting tossed out of any ball game. I felt like I was well liked by all the ballplayers; I got along with everybody. I was thankful I was able to play ball for all those years. I spent all those years in baseball and I was proud of the whole time."

He says he missed the game when he first left it. "But as time goes on you don't, because you don't know anybody anymore, except maybe an old coach or something. I watch games now on TV. I don't think I've been across the bridge ten times since moving here twenty-six years ago. I don't care for the city. It's not the same city. I used to like to go over for a show or something. But I don't even like to do that anymore."

I turn off my tape recorder and close my notebooks. Then I ask him for directions back to the turnpike. "It'd be a lot easier if you just follow me and I'll get you back on there." I follow him out to Route 46, the access to the turnpike. As we near the highway, he moves into the right lane and vigorously points left, where I am to turn. My last glimpse of him is as he turns right and, staring straight ahead, returns my wave and drives away from the sun back toward home.

WILLARD MARSHALL'S MAJOR LEAGUE CAREER

Year	Team	Games	Home Runs	RBI	BA
1942	Giants	116	11	59	.257
1946	Giants	131	13	48	.282
1947	Giants	155	36	107	.291
1948	Giants	143	14	86	.272
1949	Giants	141	12	70	.307
1950	Braves	105	5	40	.235
1951	Braves	136	11	62	.281
1952	Braves	21	2	11	.227
	Reds	107	8	46	.267
1953	Reds	122	17	62	.266
1954	White Sox	47	1	7	.254
1955	White Sox	22	0	6	.171
TOTALS		**1,246**	**130**	**604**	**.274**

WALT DROPO:

Boston Red Sox, 1950

"They [pitchers] didn't know what the hell they were doing. They thought they could strike me out with this or that. And the harder they threw, the harder I hit it, and the farther I hit it."

Nineteen-fifty American League Rookie of the Year Walt Dropo broke into the big leagues as auspiciously as anyone who ever played the game. He feasted on major league pitching, pounding thirty-four home runs and driving in a league-leading 144 runs, though he played in only 136 games. He also batted a healthy .322. It was a glorious season for the big guy from Moosup, Connecticut, who didn't make it with the Sox until he was twenty-six years old. He hung on for twelve more serviceable seasons, but never again approached the stratosphere of 1950. Yet his years away from baseball have been monetarily more fruitful than was his major league career.

He is sixty-five now, with no intention of retiring from the successful import business he operates with his brother. He has traveled widely, and was a member of the first group of businessmen to visit the People's Republic of China after President Nixon made such travel possible in 1972.

Dropo, known as "Moose" during his playing days—a monicker attributed to either his hometown or his physical stature—is still an imposing figure. He is six feet five inches tall and does not appear to weigh much more than the muscular 220 pounds he carried in his prime. His voice is a deep growl, which might easily materialize as a potent intimidating factor when he is aroused or angered.

He lives alone in a thirtieth-story penthouse on India Row in downtown Boston near the Aquarium. The view from his window of downtown Boston, the Custom House Tower, and the U.S.S. *Constitution* is magnificent. His residence is filled with oriental prints and other objets d'art: Chinese chests, vases, dried flora.

On the entry wall is a framed offprint of the *New York Times* story on his election as American League Rookie of the Year in 1950. The west wall features more baseball memorabilia, mostly photographs. There's a large aerial view of Fenway Park, and under that a montage of Dropo's baseball cards, mug shots of him wearing uniforms of all the teams he played for during his career: the Red Sox, Tigers, White Sox, Reds, and Orioles. Next to that is a color print of Dropo as a Boston player, kneeling, posing with a bat. Beneath these is a letter from the Hall of Fame thanking him for the ball he hit on July 15, 1952, his twelfth consecutive hit, which tied the major league record. There are two prominent framed photos here too, though only one is of him. It is an action shot, and he has just connected for a home run in Fenway Park. The other photo also depicts a home-run swing, but it is of Ted Williams, a man Dropo greatly respects as a hitter and as a person.

His dining room is cluttered; loose correspondence, newspapers, and books turned facedown on the table. He says he is presently reading a biography of Adolf Hitler and a book about Russia, which he anticipates visiting soon.

I have come calling on a January evening with my brother, David, an associate dean at Bentley College in nearby Waltham. David overcame his boyhood predilection for adventure stories and eventually became an avid baseball fan. For the past two decades, he's been a frequent visitor to Fenway Park. Steeped as he is in the lore and legend of Fenway and the Red Sox, David had told me he'd enjoy meeting one of the storied players from our youth.

He and Dropo immediately launch into a discussion of the Orient, which David has also recently visited. Dropo's business these days is mainly concerned with importing fireworks and garments from China.

This night, the old slugger is dressed in a rust-red crewneck sweater and beige slacks. His hair is thick and black, turning gray at the temples. He offers coffee, pours, carries a cup to the living room, settles back in a deep leather chair, and lights a cigar. "I really love the culture of the Chinese," he says, blowing a stream of smoke toward the ceiling. "Much more fascinating than the Europeans'."

David mentions that Dropo still looks fit, and Dropo grins. "Yeah, well, I work out every day I can, depending on the weather. I play a lot of golf. I love to play golf—it has a lot of the characteristics of swinging at a baseball, but a lot of people don't realize that."

He raises his coffee cup and puts the cigar in an ashtray. "I had a checkered career—a checkered life," he offers without prodding. "World War Two came along and obstructed my whole life. Like it did to DiMaggio and Williams. But they had been in the major leagues. I was at the University of Connecticut. I was a sophomore in '42, and they said if you would enroll in any one of the programs they had—you didn't have to be an athlete—they would guarantee that you would finish your collegiate career. So we just signed up for the ROTC. But in '43, we got directives from Washington—I guess Hitler was in Stalingrad or Leningrad, and we got called in. So I spent '43, '44, '45 in Germany and Italy and France. I lost those years, and in '46 I go right back to the university, and accelerated into a year and a half. Went right through, summers and everything, and got my degree. I signed in '47 with the Red Sox. So I was older then. I started my minor league career. I was very fortunate to have made it. I was twenty-six years old starting my rookie year.

"Why was I Rookie of the Year?" he asks, looking at me. I'm not sure the question is rhetorical, and cough nervously until he answers a moment later. "Because I was in the war three years. I would have been in the major leagues probably four years earlier, but I had that maturity. The war had an effect on my career early. In the minors I played at Scranton and at Birmingham and at Louisville.

"Then my rookie year I had a team that was capable of putting people on base. We had table-setters like Johnny Pesky and Dom DiMaggio and Williams. These guys could get a hundred walks and two hundred hits. That's three hundred times on base. You talk about Boggs today, well, we had three of them. We had DiMaggio, Pesky, and Williams batting ahead of me. And we had Vern Stephens [who tied Dropo that year for the league lead in RBI]. We had guys on base all the time. If you could hit at all, you had to drive in runs. But that was an exceptional year. I don't know if any other rookie had a year quite like it." He pauses and relights his cigar.

I mention that his and Stephens's combined RBI total was virtually unheard-of. "That's right," he booms. "Never been done probably in the history of baseball, that two guys drove in two hundred and eighty-eight runs in one year.

"You know, it happened so suddenly, I couldn't take it in at the time. You may not have known that I started the season in Louisville. Joe Cronin [the general manager] said they were gonna start me off there. But he said, 'Get yourself ready.' Then Billy Goodman broke his ankle, I think, the first week of the season. So I get a call to report. They told me to go to Cleveland and that I'd be in the lineup the next day. Well," he says, nodding, gesturing with his cigar, "all I needed was a break."

He took full advantage of that break by immediately going on a tear against the league's finest pitchers. "I started hitting," he said, reflecting, gazing at the ash forming on the end of his cigar. "And they couldn't get me out. They didn't know *how* to get me out. It took them the whole year before they found out." He laughs. "They didn't know what the hell they were doing. They thought they could strike me out with this or that," he says, leaning forward and indicating with his hand pitches high and tight or low and away. "And the harder they threw, the harder I hit it, and the *farther* I hit it. It was just an exciting year, a golden summer, and I can't relive it."

He pauses momentarily, draws on the cigar. "I didn't have any real prolonged slumps, except I did get hit in the head in August, and I was out a week. That's why I played in only one hundred and thirty-nine games." Actually, it was one hundred and thirty-six games according to the record books, but I don't interrupt. "I played only one hundred and thirty-nine games and drove in one hundred and forty-four runs. I drove in more runs than I played games."

Most ballplayers remember their first home run and what it meant. I ask about his.

He grins. "My first home run was off Rapid Robert Feller, right here. And I said to myself, if I can hit a home run off Feller I belong in the big leagues. I said to myself, who the hell can be better than Feller? He had a fantastic career. I said to myself, I belong here. Who's gonna stop me now? And that, more than anything else, is what got me going. This was the first or second game I played after I was called up. Yeah. I hit it in the screen in left field." He coughs, sips coffee.

"I was in a fortunate position, in the middle of the lineup. They couldn't pitch around me too well either. They had to challenge me."

He's correct. There were no easy outs in that Red Sox lineup. The team batted a lusty .302 and drove in 974 runs, leading the league in both categories. Dropo, Bobby Doerr, Stephens, and Williams all hit more than twenty homers, though Williams played only eighty-nine games because of a broken elbow. And Doerr, sandwiched between Dropo and Stephens, also managed 120 RBI.

"*Everybody* was hitting," Dropo said. "If I was a power hitter alone they might have been able to finesse me around and walk me more often. But we had Stephens in there, we had Doerr in there. So you're not just gonna pitch around me or walk me to get at those fellas."

Boston produced hits and runs in abundance that year, outscoring the pennant-winning Yankees by 1,027 runs to 914. Second-place Detroit scored only 837 runs. The Red Sox problem was pitching. No reliever had more than five saves, and the staff ERA was 4.88.

I ask him about other significant moments of 1950—any special home runs?

He thinks for a moment. "Well, I beat Raschi here with a ninth-inning home run. I hit a grand slam off of Tommy Byrne in the first inning. But you're asking me to remember something that happened forty years ago. There's lots of people who don't even live forty years. As Mantle said, 'If I knew I was gonna live this long, I'd have taken better care of myself.'" Dropo laughs, his dark eyes dance. Then he becomes somber. "Ah, he's got bad legs now."

After his momentous rookie year, sportswriters wondered if Dropo would fall victim to the dreaded sophomore slump. Early in spring training in 1951, Yankees manager Casey Stengel was asked how his club would pitch to the Moose during the coming season. The "old perfesser" issued a prophetic statement. "That Dropo can be pitched to," Stengel said. "He will not hit anywhere near as well as he did last season. High and tight and that big guy is licked. Show him the ball outside and he will murder it."

American League hurlers apparently took Stengel's advice, for Dropo's batting average tumbled to .239, and he hit only eleven home runs while driving in just fifty-eight. He appeared in only ninety-nine games, and spent part of the season back on the Louisville farm. However, his offensive production in 1951 was hampered by the broken wrist he suffered on April 2. I ask him how the injury affected his play that disastrous season.

He leans forward in his seat. "I never used that as an excuse, but I have to tell you in retrospect that like any injury, when you're dealing with your wrist . . ." He holds up his left arm and touches the ulna. "Your reflex, coordination, your timing, sense of quickness with the bat, psychologically—it's a whole thing that goes through your mind." He slumps back in his chair. "I struggled all year long.

"I may have tried to come back too soon. I think so." He flexes his wrist now, back and forth, back and forth, makes a circle with it. "I did everything wrong. That was just a bad year. I said I was okay. It was a hairline fracture, but my tendons must have been involved. Who knows? It wasn't a major, crippling type of thing, but when you're talking about hitting a hundred-mile-an-hour fastball, your hands—I mean, it woulda been better if I had broken my leg. Six weeks in a cast, and after that I'd have been all right. This has an effect on your quickness with the bat."

The old first baseman stands and takes his stance, makes one, two practice swings from his crouch. He straightens and leans back, reliving again the pitch that sidelined him. "I fell away from a pitch, and it hit me right there"—he touches the ulna—"and fractured it." He studies his wrist. "I know exactly where it hit that bone. Cracked it. I gotta tell you, it was an awful struggle. It wasn't the injury so much, it was my getting back in the groove, swinging the way I did before. I tell you, I worked all that winter long to get back in shape.

"But," he says, sighing, "the psychology of the fifties was you'd better play. Like old Satchel Paige would say, 'Don't look back, there's somebody waiting to take your job.' There's somebody always gaining on you. So we were always in a position where we wanted to play. We never wanted to sit out."

Instead of sitting out, the big guy was sent down to the minors to try to recapture his stroke. By the end of June he'd hit only four homers and was batting only .230 in the friendly confines of Fenway Park. The previous year, he'd hit .374 in Fenway. He was recalled by the Red Sox on July 28 and finished the season with them.

By 1952, Lou Boudreau, the new Sox manager, thought Dick Gernert could take over at first base, and Dropo was traded to Detroit, where he would enjoy something of a comeback. 1952 would be his second-best season in the big leagues, as he hit twenty-nine homers and batted in ninety-seven runs. But most significantly, he tied Pinky Higgins's major league record for consecutive hits. Because it is a record, noting one of baseball's hottest streaks, Dropo enjoys talking about it.

"It started in Yankee Stadium," he says. "I'm not sure, but I think it was Raschi who started the ball game. Geez, that's twenty-seven years ago. I should remember every one of them, but I don't. I think it was Raschi or Jim McDonald who started the game. In New York I went five for five. That was on Saturday. On Sunday, July fourteenth, we went to Washington to play the Senators in a doubleheader. The pitcher was Walt Masterson. I got four hits off Masterson, and then I hit against Bob Porterfield and Lou Slater in the next game. I got three hits and tied the record off Slater, but then he got me out. I got a hit or two after that too. I think in that stretch I went fourteen for fifteen, and that's another record."

For those three games Dropo was the hottest hitter in major league baseball history. He was experiencing what author John Jerome calls "the sweet spot in time," where he could do no wrong. Those moments are difficult for athletes to analyze, though most try, and Walt Dropo gives it a shot.

"You don't know why it happens to you," he says, picking up his cigar. It has grown cold and he puts it down again. "You don't know why you go into a slump. Physically, psychologically, mentally, you're ready. I know after those five consecutive hits I had in New York, I could have gone out and celebrated. But I knew we had a doubleheader the next day and I was tired. I went to bed early that night. I was very excited because I had five in a row, and I knew I was in a hot streak, and I just wanted to rest. . . . You get in that groove. I don't care what they threw at me, I always seemed to get good wood on it—line drives. I didn't hit any home runs out of the twelve, so that means I was swinging parallel—making good contact. I didn't change anything. I had no idea about any record until I came up there and the public address announcer said I was approaching the record. And that made me a little tense.

"You know, the media at that time wasn't like it is today. When you get close to a record they start chasing you. But nobody had a chance to get to me, because this happened so fast—a couple days. Three games and two days. Maris's sixty-one homers has a connotation that's entirely different. He went through hell with that thing. Reporters are around your locker after every game. It's tough enough to go up there and get a base hit. They didn't do it intentionally, but it's the media on top of you. Nobody ever knew about mine, it happened so quickly. There are only two or three records like that. Don Larsen's perfect no-hitter in the series, and Johnny Vandermeer's back-to-back no-hitters. But the one that gets all the attention is DiMaggio's fifty-six-game hitting streak. Gets all the accolades. Now Joe D deserves all the attention, but every time they start bringing up the records, it's Joe D, Joe D. Like nobody else set any records. Vandermeer's record is like mine—instantaneous things that just happened.

"Whatever they threw at me, I didn't care what it was. I never could see the spin on the ball or the seams, but I could pick up the rotation. That ball's traveling ninety miles an hour. Not easy to see it at that speed. Like a bullet or a shot coming at you. To make contact with the ball, your hand-to-eye acuity has to be there. I think Williams had it more so than anyone else. He was quicker than the average. And by quicker, I don't mean we're saying this is a curve, a slider, but rather it's just like boom-boom-boom." He snaps his fingers with each "boom." "A fraction of a second.

"Now one time in New York, I was hitting behind Williams and Allie Reynolds was pitching. First time up, he got Williams out. Ted came back and said to me, 'Be careful now. He's quick today.' He's alerting me that Reynolds today is sensitive, quicker. Now how much more could this be than the time before when he pitched against us? All he says is be ready. That's all I need to hear. That if he got in a jam and threw me a fastball, I gotta be ready. That's enough. That's how we talked to each other. A definition within ourselves as to the speed of the ball. Is he quick today? Or is he throwing a lot of shit, a lot of slop up there? Or is he smoking?"

During the fourteen-for-fifteen streak, though, it was Dropo who was smoking, lining pitches all over the field. Of those twelve straight hits, only a double and a triple went for extra bases. Five RBI were produced in that string.

Relighting his cigar, he resumes speaking, the stogie clamped between his teeth. "When I was hot, I hit anything. Any pitcher, any pitch. But you gotta start defining what is a pitcher." He points toward his window, and the lights on "Old Ironsides." "Hoyt Wilhelm couldn't break that pane of glass if he threw as hard as he could. But he threw that crazy knuckleball. He could throw it all day long." Dropo indicates the erratic movement of the knuckler, moving his hand up and down, back and forth. "That's like hitting a butterfly.

"Then you had the hard throwers like Score, Reynolds, Feller. Guys like Bob Lemon threw nothing but hard sliders and hard sinkers. When the slider came along, it took a guy away from his sweet spot. And that's the whole purpose of a slider. It will take you away from that sweet spot in your bat. About this far." He holds his hands about six inches apart. "Now that's the key to the slider. So the batter might miss a curveball, but hey, he'll maybe hit the slider, but he won't hit it hard, and he'll hit it on the ground. So Lemon threw sinkers in on you and sliders this way." He indicates a pitch low and away. "He had you going both ways. You were always on the defensive. And that's a very difficult type of pitcher to hit.

"Whitey Ford was another type. Similar in character, only he'd start you out one way one time, and he'd start you out another way another time. He'd start you out with a curveball outside, then he starts you with a curveball inside. Then he sets you up and you're looking inside, outside, and you're hesitating." Here Dropo pantomimes the batter's dilemma: looking for the outside pitch, then flinching when the ball buzzes beneath his chin. "He might give you the fastball, but you hesitated that fraction of a second, and he's got you. It was like a chess game with him. You couldn't get that bat on the ball. He took the bat right out of your hands.

"Everybody says, well, cripes, anybody can hit Whitey Ford, gimme the bat. What they don't realize is what he had. He had strict control of every pitch he threw. Whitey Ford was one of the toughest guys I ever faced. For that reason, not because of the velocity of his pitches. When we're talking about velocity, we're talking about Score, Sandy Koufax. First inning, boom-boom-boom, he's throwing and striking everybody out. But I figure, wait a minute. Maybe by the seventh inning, he loses a little something, and then I can time him. I gotta keep him clocked, and maybe when a little got off that fastball—pow." He is standing, pantomiming a healthy swing. "That's all you could hope for. Don't worry about him striking you out the first time up and maybe the second time up. You got four shots at him.

"You might have a great day against a guy once, and the next time you see him it's entirely different. There was never a pitcher in either league that you consistently wore out, otherwise he'd be gone. Believe me." He pauses to finish off the cold dregs of his coffee, then sits. "In those days we didn't have computers fine-tuned to tell you what you did every time against a certain pitcher."

When he's on a roll, Dropo's animated speech erupts, gets ahead of his audience, and sometimes, it seems, ahead of himself. I break in on him and ask him about the trade that took him from Boston to Detroit. I'd heard about the Red Sox mystique, that virtually every player who was with Boston always considered himself first and foremost a Red Sox player, even after being traded several times over, and even if his career in Boston had been relatively brief. Dropo spent more time with the Tigers and White Sox than with Boston. Yet in his mind, and in the minds of most fans, he remains a former Red Sox first baseman.

The trade upset him at the time, he said. "But now I look at it and it was probably the greatest thing that ever happened to me. 'Cause I learned to play baseball—and not just look at that wall out there." He's speaking, of course, of the left-field fence in Fenway, otherwise known as the Green Monster. "Now I knew I could play in any ballpark. I played in big ballparks. I probably would have had better stats here, but I think if I'd stayed here, I'd have swung for those fences all the time. That has an effect on you. It hurt a lot of guys. It hurt Jackie Jensen, it hurt Stephens. You go on the road, and it's very difficult to shift gears and hit in Yankee Stadium." He turns in his seat, crosses his long legs. "It's a strange wall," he says, referring to the Green Monster. "It's a monster. I loved it. It had some great psychological aspects to it—the feeling you can reach it even if you don't hit the ball that well. On the other hand, you hit a line drive that you think might be a home run, it hits the wall and you end up with only a single. You're in constant conflict with yourself. It's a strange phenomenon, that wall."

I ask him if he felt his first-year stats were going to haunt him after he completed his rookie season. Did he feel pressure to always measure up to what he achieved in 1950?

He exhales a cloud of blue smoke. "The media and the fans had those expectations," he begins deliberately. "I knew what my capabilities were as a ballplayer. What I performed in thirteen years is what I really was. I was a .270 hitter, and the reason was I was a right-handed hitter with no speed. So what I did, I think, was a good accomplishment. In other words, you look at that, and then the pitchers too, and after a while they start to catch on to you. They realize they're not gonna challenge me in here all the time." He runs his hand across his chest, indicating the inside corner of the plate. "They learned after a while they're not gonna get away with that. So it was give and take until we settled down. And when the dust settled after thirteen years, that's what you got. I'm proud of my record. I'm not Mantle or DiMaggio, or Willie Mays, or you know—they're a different level of player. But I'm in the run of the mill with guys like Kluzewski, Hodges, guys like that. You could put us on in one package—we're not that far apart."

But did those fan and media expectations mess up his mind?

"No." His answer is immediate. "After I left here, I became more of a total ballplayer. Especially when I got to the White Sox. We had the go-go kids, Aparicio, Fox, Rivera, Minoso, Kell—and we had a good ball club. We were solid, and we could win the pennant. And we played every game as though we could win, and there wasn't any power. I learned to play the game the way it should be played. You may win a game three-two or two-one; you're not gonna pound the daylights out of somebody. All the time pulverizing them, which we did here. It becomes a more interesting game that way. I enjoyed it more."

Dropo enjoyed all sports, and played football and basketball as well as baseball at the University of Connecticut. A gifted all-around athlete, he was drafted by pro teams in all three sports before settling on baseball, which he found more challenging. "In baseball, the concentration level is high-intensity, and involves a high level of skill. There's only ten thousand or so ex–major leaguers. How many have tried to play? We are in a very, very select group. Everyone who made it to the major leagues I put in one category, whether they're Mantle or DiMaggio or just got into one game. In that framework there is an intensity beyond the average fan's understanding of it. The average fan does not understand what is required to hit a major league pitcher. Williams made the statement that it is the most difficult art or skill in any sport. I endorse it, because I've played 'em all. Football is nothing compared to hitting a baseball. Football requires different skills. You gotta be able to stand." He gets up, assumes the position of a defensive end, which he played, and charges across any imaginary line of scrimmage. "You gotta be quick. But have the acuity to stand there and hit—I mean the intensity is such that . . ." He lets the thought drift away, while he returns to his chair. "I remember Williams used to say, standing up there in batting practice, 'Jesus Christ can't throw the fastball by me.' Now that's an attitude. That the Lord, the Messiah, can't throw the sonombitch by me. Throw as hard as you want. Now there's an attitude.

"So that is the attitude in our level of thinking. That makes you a great hitter. You say to yourself, no sonombitch gonna throw the ball by me. I don't care if it's Koufax, if it's Drysdale, you name it. He can't throw the ball by me. You gotta believe, and that's attitude. I knew I could hit a major league fastball. That didn't bother me. What bothered me was settin' me up.

"Because I've heard guys say, 'Eddie Lopat? You can't hit that?' I'd like to see *them* go up there and hit against Eddie Lopat and try to figure out what Eddie Lopat's doin' to them." He's standing again, agitated as he pantomimes the way pitches looked to a batter from the old Yankee hurler's repertoire. "They wouldn't get the bat anywhere near the ball.

"Lopat now, he probably kept me in here." He draws a high, tight pitch. "It's not hard throwing, but it's the game we're playing that the average fan doesn't understand. There's a man on first base in the eighth inning, and you don't want to hit a ground ball because it takes our team out of the inning. All these elements are factored in. The average layman doesn't understand what I'm talking about."

Walt Dropo played his last game in the big leagues in 1961 with the Baltimore Orioles. He'd been sharing first base with the young Jim Gentile. "I was a right-handed hitter, and Gentile was left-handed. They were grooming him to take over first base. My career ended in Minneapolis. Gentile hit a grand slam in the first inning, and they brought a left-hander in and he stayed in the game and hit a grand slam off the left-hander. So they decided to go with him full-time. And that was the end of my career. When we got back home, Lee McPhail called and said, 'We're gonna have to release you.' He was very good about it. I was thirty-eight years old and I didn't have any resentments. I had a good career, I had no regrets. I have no regrets about the salaries they're getting today, the pensions they're getting today. By the grace of God it could be me there today. But I had my moments of glory, like you said. I had some other compensations for it also. We're recognized by the fans. I think the fifties were the golden years. There were only eight teams in each league. The game wasn't watered-down, and to get to the big leagues you had to be better qualified, better grounded in fundamentals." He goes to the kitchen and refills his coffee cup.

As he does so, I probe him about the contemporary game. What does he like or dislike most about baseball today?

He returns from the kitchen. "I'm away from baseball now," he says. "I'm in the garment business, the fireworks business. I'm a little active in golf. I don't get over to Fenway that often anymore. I have difficulty sitting through a ball game. You know, I'm not a spectator. I'm a participant. They're two different animals. I can't even watch it on TV. I have no vicarious thrill out of it. It doesn't do anything for me. What can I get out of watching a ball game on television? Seeing the mistakes they're making that you can't see? I have no interest in it."

What he is interested in, these days, is business, and travel related to business. He's a salesman, and he loves the challenge of direct sales, the hard-sell approach.

"Sure, I used baseball as an entry into the business world," he tells me. "It opens doors, but then you're on your own. I was in the investment business with IDS. Greatest training I ever got was with IDS. Now everything is computerized, but in our day we sat down with you and had to convince you that you needed a retirement plan, or increase your insurance, that you had to put money away. It was a hard, hard sell. Doctors would let me in and say, 'What makes you think I should buy insurance from you just because you're Walter Dropo?' That's a lesson that you got. It isn't the presentation, because anybody can make a presentation. I got every objection covered. The question is why he should buy it from you. And if he doesn't, it's the rejection that hurts more than the fact that he doesn't buy. He rejected *you*. See, before everybody's coming to *you* for an autograph—sign here, sign here. Now I'm turning around and asking you to sign a contract with me. And the fact that you don't do it—you can't take it personally. You learn after a while and you go to the next stop. But starting out, you take it personally. I made it on a commission basis only. You were paid if you made a sale." He's very animated again. 'See, somewhere along the line the customer pays. You might as well tell him right up front." He stops, exhales slowly.

"Ah, but that was another war, another career. I'll tell you this, though, it was almost as rewarding as baseball."

David and I stand to leave, and Walter Dropo walks us to the door. I thank him for his time. "It was fun," he says, shaking hands. "Baseball was a skill. God gave you talent. But you gotta have desire too. Desire and determination takes over. The skill's gotta be inbred in you. I was an athlete. I was a better athlete than Williams. Sure, he could hit a lot better than I could," he says, smiling. "And he could fish better too, but that's not a sport." He laughs.

"I could play football, I could play basketball, I could play baseball. I was big, I was strong. I was everything. I could do everything; I could coordinate my body. The easiest thing to do in the world is evaluate talent. Anybody can do that." We are now standing in the hallway, and Dropo's voice is booming, bouncing off walls and into adjacent apartments. One tenant opens her door a crack to see if there's a commotion. But it's only her huge neighbor telling anecdotes to a couple of visitors. Dropo does not seem to notice her standing there. I do, and start to ease away, not certain that Dropo is ready to conclude his monologue. "The main thing," he continues, "is heart. Desire. You cannot put that in somebody's computer." He pauses, smiles. He's finished. "There," he says. "That oughta do it, okay?" He backs into his apartment, the door clicks shut. His neighbor eases into the hallway and watches as David and I board the elevator to the lobby.

WALT DROPO'S MAJOR LEAGUE CAREER

Year	Team	Games	Home Runs	RBI	BA
1949	Red Sox	11	0	1	.146
1950	Red Sox	136	34	144	.322
1951	Red Sox	99	11	57	.239
1952	Red Sox	37	6	27	.265
	Tigers	115	23	70	.279
1953	Tigers	152	13	96	.248
1954	Tigers	107	4	44	.281
1955	White Sox	141	19	79	.280
1956	White Sox	125	8	52	.266
1957	White Sox	93	13	49	.256
1958	White Sox	28	2	8	.192
	Reds	63	7	31	.290
1959	Reds	26	1	2	.103
	Orioles	62	6	21	.268
1960	Orioles	79	4	21	.268
1961	Orioles	14	1	2	.270
TOTALS		**1,288**	**152**	**704**	**.270**

NED GARVER:

St. Louis Browns, 1951

*"The ball club had a lot of confidence in me. . . . I
pitched quickly, threw strikes, and the defense was
sharper. . . . I didn't fool around out there. I just
pitched."*

The cold is bone-chilling on this brilliant, sunny afternoon four
days before Christmas. Hillocks of gleaming virgin snow have
drifted over the cornfields that line either side of Highway 15 as
it winds south from the Ohio Turnpike. All of Defiance County
looks like a picture postcard: the smooth new snow set off by
bright red barns and silos, some bearing the large advertisement:
CHEW MAIL POUCH TOBACCO.

In this bucolic setting, I'm rather surprised to hear on my car
radio a small-town station play June Christy's recording of "I Fall
in Love Too Easily." But then, rural America has never been as
regressive as is often assumed by outsiders. And I didn't really
expect to hear only nasal twanging country tunes once out of the
range of major-market stations.

I'm heading for a village called Ney, the lifelong residence of

Ned Garver, who in 1951 recorded one of baseball's most astounding pitching feats by winning twenty games for the perennially hapless St. Louis Browns. The Browns won only fifty-four games and lost one hundred, finishing, as was their custom, in the American League cellar. No other pitcher before or since has ever won twenty games for a team that has lost a hundred games in a season.

Ney (population 325) is located some thirty miles from both Toledo and Fort Wayne and is about twenty miles south of the turnpike. It is where Ned Garver grew up, and the place where he returned when his playing career ended during the 1961 season. Since then, he's farmed briefly, but retired in 1980 from a public relations job with a meatpacking firm in nearby Defiance. He's served his village seven years as its mayor since returning home, and has never been off the town council.

He is sixty-four years old when we meet, no longer the chunky, baby-faced kid who was clearly baseball's best pitcher during that unusual 1951 season. That year was unique both for Garver's remarkable 20–12 record and for the disruption caused when Browns owner Bill Veeck, borrowing from James Thurber's story "You Could Look It Up," hired Eddie Gaedel, who stood three feet seven, as a pinch hitter.

Though we will not discuss Gaedel, or Veeck's penchant for showmanship, it is clear that Garver was and remains a man serious about baseball and his role in the sport.

His sprawling home is at the end of Water Street, set back a good half-block from the road, on a seven-and-a-half-acre lot that used to be part of his father's farm. It is decorated for the season. Eight stockings hang from the mantel. The fireplace has been given a wood-stove insert, and there's a roaring fire warming the room as I enter.

Garver still carries his playing-days physique—five feet ten and perhaps 190 pounds, which is slightly more than he weighed when he played. He needs glasses now, but his hair is still dark-running-to-gray. He settles into a rocking chair near the front window in his living room and folds his hands in his lap.

In addition to his spectacular 1951 season, Ned Garver was also the first major league player to challenge baseball's reserve clause, though credit for opening up free agency is usually attributed to Curt Flood. After the 1951 season, however, Garver sent a letter to the New York Representative Emmanuel Cellar, who conducted an investigation into contracts that bound players to teams for life at the discretion of teams owning the contracts.

I don't remember much about this, and as I find a chair near an outlet for my tape recorder, I ask him about it.

"Well, as I remember it, Curt Flood was challenging the reserve clause, and of course I was paying attention to it. But I didn't see any proposal they were making that would be an adequate substitution for the reserve clause. I thought when I played that if a person stayed with a ball club and didn't get a chance to play over a reasonable period of time—like those folks who played catcher behind Yogi Berra all those years—they'd have to trade you or release you." He chuckles. "Curt Flood and those people just wanted to do away with the reserve clause and weren't proposing anything as an adequate substitute. So when they asked me to testify in Washington in behalf of this, I refused.

"I mean, an organization that has signed you, given you an opportunity to play and develop to get to be a major leaguer in the first place, it seems to me, is entitled to some consideration.

"Now that letter I sent to Cellar, I don't even remember what I wrote, because I didn't keep a copy of it."

I remind him that Cellar reported that if Garver had been with a first-division team he'd have been worth $90,000 to $100,000 per year. With the lowly Browns his top salary was $25,000—which happens to be the highest salary ever paid a player on the old franchise before it moved to Baltimore. At one time Bill Veeck reportedly turned down $390,000 for Garver—an offer that doubtless would have increased Garver's baseball earnings. Attendance was always sparse in St. Louis.

He smiles slightly as I mention this. "Well now, a lot of that was supposition. I won forty-five games in a three-year span with the Browns. I was never knocked out of the last nineteen games I started for them. In 1951 I completed twenty-four games, which was a major portion of the games I started. People were sayin' if you were with the Yankees, instead of winning thirteen or fourteen games, you'd have won twenty, and then in 1951 when you won twenty, you might have won thirty." He chuckles again. "That's problematical, because the manager has to use you in a different way. Now Casey Stengel would pull his pitchers when they were having a bad day. He'd quick get them out of there. That protects your earned run average. It protects a win too, if a long reliever holds the lead. In my case I very seldom pitched a game I didn't get credit for one way or the other. I either won it or lost it. And a lot of them were lost."

I mention that perhaps he wasn't quickly removed from the mound in 1951 because he swung a pretty good bat. He hit .305 that year, and often pinch-hit during his career.

He smiles. "Yeah. I was used a lot as a pinch hitter. Never got paid anything extra for it. I hit .400 that year as a pinch hitter. I hit sixth in the lineup a good percentage of the time. I hit .288 one other season. I tell you, I got knocked down a few times, and came awful close to getting hit. I'd bear down in certain circumstances, but other times, I was gonna protect myself. Try to keep from gettin' hurt. In those days we didn't have the specialists they do now, so I suppose I was allowed to stay in a lot of ball games."

1951, though, was clearly the highwater mark of Garver's major league career. Toiling for so wretched a team, how could he manage to win twenty games?

He shrugs. "The ball club had a lot of confidence in me. My people felt we had a good chance to win when I pitched. I had established myself as a guy who could pitch when we were ahead, when we were behind, or whatever. In other words, some pitchers could pitch when they were tied or one run behind, or when they were ahead. But in the seventh inning a pitcher gives up two runs and you've got to take him out. I had proven over time that you get me a couple runs, I'm likely to win. They had confidence in me. I pitched quickly, threw strikes, and the defense was sharper. They liked that. I didn't fool around out there. I just pitched. They like to play those games in less than two hours, and you get things moving along. My defense played well because of confidence.

"You always gotta fight against a losing attitude. If you think you're gonna get beat, you probably will." He pauses, his hands still folded on his lap. His eyes narrow and he is on the road to reminiscence. "I remember pitching one time in the Texas League and a guy got a single to center. I couldn't believe it. I threw the ball right where I wanted to throw it and expected to get him out. I was really shocked. I remember once throwing a ball, and Les Moss was gonna catch it on the outside corner right down here." He is standing, drawing an imaginary home plate with his hand, and indicating where Moss anticipated the pitch—down and away. "Joe DiMaggio hit it over the scoreboard in Sportsman's Park for a home run. Not many folks could do that, pull my slider and hit it out of the park. If they're gonna hit that slider good, they're gonna hit it to the opposite field. But when you're playing people with that kind of ability, they surprise you. Hank Aaron [whom Garver faced only in spring exhibition games] was something. Sometimes I thought I got the ball by him, and son of a biscuit if he wouldn't hit the ball—a bullet into right center field. He'd wait on the ball," Garver says, pantomiming now, "and boom—he's quick with the bat. Not very many hitters like that, and thank goodness." He laughs.

One thing I've wondered about prior to visiting Garver is whether he resented playing for second-division teams through-out his career. Not once in his fourteen years did he ever play for a winner. I mention this, and the corners of his mouth turn downward for an instant.

"I never resented that, and I don't dwell on it," he says. "And I'm not sympathetic to players about that now. A ball club gave them the opportunity, but they feel sorry for themselves, making far more money than they could doing anything else, and yet they're feeling sorry because they're not with the team that wins. They destroy the competitiveness of the league.

"However, I do say this: if you played in a World Series, people get the impression that you were somewhat more of an outstanding player than if you never did. You're put in a kind of special category if you were on a pennant-winning team. I would have loved being on a winner too, but I don't see how I can feel sorry for myself, because I got to play in the major leagues. If I'd been with New York or Cleveland, I'd have been in the minor leagues a lot longer, because they had great players. I'd have been behind some of those outstanding people there.

"I had chances to go with someone else. There were four teams after me when I pitched in the national amateur tournament in Youngstown. If I'd been smart I'd have sized them all up, but my coach was sort of bird-dogging for St. Louis and I asked him if he could line me up a job with them. And he did. This was at the end of 1943. I went to spring training with the Browns in 1944."

Garver started the 1944 season with the Toledo Mudhens in the American Association, but fearful he wouldn't stick around long, asked to be sent somewhere near his home. He was deposited in Newark, Ohio, in the Class D Ohio State League. He says that demotion was critical to his success in pro baseball. "I won twenty-four games that year and hit .407. I pinch-hit and played outfield, and believe it or not, drove in more runs than our catcher." He laughs. "I had a 1.21 ERA, which was the lowest earned run average in all of baseball that year. And that was important. You should always play at a level where you can experience some success. You can always look back on that when things are rough and know you did it once so you should be able to be successful again."

He was back at Toledo the next year, but recalls with some bitterness how management—citing a technicality in his contract—deprived him of a $500 bonus.

"It was in my contract that if I stayed with the team the entire season I'd get an extra five hundred dollars. Well, the team was about to go on a ten-day road trip, but I was told that Elmira needed some pitching—this was late in the season—so they could make it into the playoffs. So I pitched a few times up there, but they didn't need pitching. All they had was pitchers. They didn't have a chance to make the playoffs either. That was a lie. I played left field every day I didn't pitch. Then Toledo called me back when they were in Louisville, and I pitched three times the last week of the season. I pitched thirty-some times for them that year. But they beat me out of the five hundred dollars by sending me to Elmira."

He spent the next two seasons pitching for San Antonio in the old Texas League, winning seventeen games his second season for a club that finished last. Once more he encountered what he maintains was an unethical management. "I won seventeen games for that last-place team, and I couldn't make any money so I went to the front office and asked for a raise. They said they had just talked to the Browns and told me I'd be called up to the big leagues at the end of San Antone's season. 'You'll have a month in the big leagues at a minimum salary over a thousand dollars.'

"I can remember their office was up a flight of stairs, and I just floated down those steps. I was so thrilled to be going to the big leagues. Not only would I get a chance to make a little more money, but I'd be up *there*." His hands, no longer folded in his lap, rest on his knees, and he is sitting forward, animated in his recollection.

"Son of a gun, came the last of August, and I hadn't heard

anything from Bill DeWitt [president of the Browns], and right after Labor Day we ended our season in Shreveport. So I wired DeWitt, and I said, 'Where am I supposed to meet you?' He wired back that I was to meet them next spring. Now that was another dirty trick." The hurt is still in his voice as he relates the incident. But Garver was a feisty competitor and wasn't about to take what he perceived as unfair treatment. "See first, they beat me out of five hundred dollars up at Toledo, and now they beat me out of money down in San Antone, plus the chance to get my feet wet in the big leagues."

Deeply hurt and frustrated, Garver took the unusual step of writing to Commissioner Happy Chandler, complaining of his victimization. He never received a response from Chandler's office; instead he got a letter from the Browns stating that the commissioner had sent them a copy of Garver's letter.

He shakes his head, still amazed that his letter would be sent on to DeWitt. "To give the letter to the St. Louis Browns, that's *unbelievable*. It is, but that's exactly what happened." He is silent for several long seconds; clearly he's never fully recovered from the frustration of having a confidence breeched by baseball's commissioner more than forty years earlier.

"Well," he says, settling back in his chair, hands folded once more, "I went up the next year in 1948 to training in San Bernardino in California, and I never went to the minor leagues after that. Almost fourteen years. I stayed there once I got there."

As a rookie for Zack Taylor's Brownies, Garver won seven games, lost eleven, and posted a highly creditable 3.41 ERA. The next year he was 12–17, and in 1950 he went 13–18.

Meanwhile, the Browns, a floundering collection of no-names and cast-offs from other clubs, continued mired in the nether depths of the American League. In 1951, they finished forty-six games out of first place, despite Garver's remarkable personal record.

I ask him if there was anything specific that stood out about 1951 as he was going through it.

He laughs. "Everything that could go right did go right. When you play with a team that loses a hundred out of a hundred and fifty-four games, you're accustomed to seeing a lot of things go wrong, but not too much go right. And when you pitch as well as the other pitchers and you lose, you didn't have a good supporting cast. The Yankees had an excellent player at every position. A lot of times with us, we'd have an outfielder playing third, or an outfielder playing first. You need to have experts at every position if you're gonna have a winning team.

"But that year, 1951, if I didn't pitch well, we got a bunch of runs. Things went well for me. And I got a couple victories in relief. I won a game one day against the Senators when I pitched nine innings and gave up seventeen hits. Now, I wasn't hit hard that day, but they hit high choppers or little pop-ups that just fell in. But we scored runs and were always leading in the game. We won that game, I think, nine–eight. Now how many times is that gonna happen? Another thing, they left me in the whole game. 'Course, we didn't have any relief specialists. But think how many pitches I must have thrown in that game." There's a long pause as he calculates. He doesn't come up with a figure, but continues, "I don't think I was ever behind in that game, so there wouldn't be any reason to take me out, would there? We don't know if we got anybody better down in the bullpen, and they're not really smokin' the ball anyhow. But it totals up, seventeen hits, eight runs. It wasn't the kind of a game you'd expect to get a win for, but that year, I got a win."

He stands, goes to the large cherry woodbox filled with firewood, removes a fresh log, and pops it in the stove. He crouches before the open stove momentarily, watching the fire as the new log catches flame, hisses, crackles. He offers a satisfied grunt and returns to his seat.

I ask if he thought 1951 would be a standard season for him.

He was only twenty-five years old, completing his fourth year in the major leagues, had been the American League starting pitcher in the All-Star game, and might look forward to ten more banner seasons.

"I expected to win," he states emphatically, leaning forward. "Now I want to tell you the truth, if I hadn't gotten hurt, I really believe I'd be in Cooperstown. I really believe it. I started the '52 season, and I shut out the Tigers and the White Sox in my first two starts. I was on top of my game. I shut out the Tigers in the opening-day game, and my next start I shut out the White Sox. That's the way I would start that season. I'll tell you something, that was just duck soup. I *know* I'm going to do pretty well. I don't *think* I'm going to do well.

"Then a couple days after I shut out the White Sox, I'm throwing batting practice for some other pitchers, and some others were out there shagging and throwing the ball back to the mound. Well, I threw a ball, and it felt to me like whoever was shagging in the outfield had thrown the ball back in and hit me right in the neck. It just *whumph*." He reaches back and touches his neck. "So after I got out of baseball I had it operated on."

I asked what had happened.

"Oh, it was a disk," he says, matter-of-factly. "It was herniated and pressed on the nerve." He touches the area near where the cervical disk had ruptured. "Anyway, the next game I pitched, I had another shutout going until about the seventh inning. Next day I couldn't straighten out my arm."

He shows me, crooking his pitching arm at about a 30-degree angle. "That was about as far as it would go. By the next time it was my turn to start there in Boston, I could straighten out the arm all right, but before the game even started it felt like I'd already pitched about ten innings. The nerves to the arm should have been getting attention, but nobody bothered. And after about five innings I ran out of gas.

"Then they take me to have my elbow X-rayed. I wasn't smart

enough to call a halt to that. There were some great trainers, but most of them were afraid for their jobs and beholden to management. They would not say 'This guy needs more attention,' because according to the X-rays, there was nothing wrong with the elbow. But instead of them saying they need to keep looking, I kept trying to pitch. And it just kept getting worse." He chuckles without humor. "I wasn't smart enough to know you just don't keep trying to pitch."

He was able to keep trying, he tells me, because he wasn't feeling significant pain. Primarily, he says, his arm felt tired, lifeless. "My breaking ball's not sharp, and finally they traded me in August to Detroit. And I pitched one game there. I went over on the fourteenth of August and on the seventeenth I pitched against the Browns and won five–two. And I want to tell you something, that last inning I pitched, I'd throw the ball and those muscles were so tired that they'd cramp like this." He holds his hand in an exaggerated claw, with fingers pressing in toward his palm and locking. He pushes his hand against his thigh to show how he worked out the cramps to grip the ball for another pitch.

"I'd do this to work out the spasm and then I could throw again. That's how stupid I was. And then for the rest of the season I couldn't throw. So at the end of the season I went to a doctor who turned that elbow and when he did it just snapped and popped. Just scared the devil out of me. I thought he broke my arm. But what he did was broke those adhesions around the elbow that had developed there. And then he put me on some sort of traction that pulled my neck, and it relieved the pressure. Over the winter I took treatment and massage and soaked in hot water every single night. And before Christmas, that feeling in my elbow disappeared."

I watch him as he tenderly, unconsciously touches his right elbow with his left hand. He looks at me, folds his hands again. "I got back, but I was never the same. I won fourteen games one year with Detroit [14–11, 1954], and I'd win eleven or twelve, something like that. 'Course, we were never a first-division team. I never played on a first-division team." He pauses, and speaks again, his voice softer. "I always dreamed of being a starting pitcher in a World Series. But I started an All-Star game, and if you're not with good teams, why . . ." He stops in mid-thought, thinking again about what might have been. Then he looks up, at the stove, back to me. "Well, you're just not likely to start a World Series game."

Still, he says he has few regrets about his career, in which he won 129 games while losing 157 from 1948 through 1961. Sure, there remain the irritations over management's beating him out of money he felt he'd earned, but in current disputes over modern player salaries, he takes management's side. If anything about his time in the big leagues rankles him, it's the failure of the baseball writers to give him the Most Valuable Player award after his splendid 1951 season.

I recall that he finished second in the balloting that year to Yogi Berra, but wasn't planning to ask about it. He brings it up himself as we near the end of the interview, as I'm wondering whether to insert a new tape in the recorder or just finish off with what I already have. He has spent the last several minutes casting worried glances out the window, frowning at gathering clouds which begin to drop more snow. His wife, Dorothy, is shopping in Fort Wayne, and she's been expected to arrive home before now. I suspect I may have overstayed my welcome, but as he turns from the window, he starts in again.

"That MVP award in 1951, now that was a dirty trick. There was no Cy Young Award then, as you may know. The New York writers decided to leave me off their ballot entirely, so that I wouldn't get any points. They didn't give me *any*. I'd already been called by the United Press or Associated Press in Cleveland and told I'd won. Because I was so far ahead. Next morning they called again and told me what happened. The New York writers wanted a local guy, so they got Yogi, and left me off the ballot." He pauses, frowning slightly. "I would love to be able to look on that roster and see Ruth, Gehrig, Jimmy Foxx, Greenberg, and then see me in there. Coming in second, that was nothing. But I'm glad I had that outstanding year. I thought I had other outstanding years, but I just didn't have the luck. I was a good pitcher. That's not bragging. If I'd have been with a good ball club, I'd probably have won more games."

Of that there's little doubt. His career ERA was a solid 3.73. He was a control pitcher who made batters hit harmless ground balls and pop-ups. Few hitters put solid wood on the ball when Garver took the mound. Now nearly thirty years after he tossed his last pitch in the big leagues, he is sitting before the wood stove in this pleasant, Christmassy setting dwelling on a past career that credits him with only one hugely successful season, that could just as easily have included six or eight great years had he played on winning teams and not herniated that cervical disk.

I unplug my recorder and close my notebooks. I reach for my coat. As an afterthought I mention that there are no baseball memorabilia in this room, and I wonder if he has any. Mementoes have been rather prominent in the homes of other former players I've visited.

He rises. "I've got a couple," he says. "But that doesn't get very high priority in our lives. That's over." Then he beckons me to follow him downstairs to the rec room in his basement. "Not many folks get down here," he says, turning on lights. On the paneled walls are photos of him in the uniforms of all the major league teams he played on. There's one of him with Bing Crosby, another with Satchel Paige, who was a longtime friend. There's the shot of him with Casey Stengel, Eddie Sawyer, and Robin Roberts—managers and starting pitchers for the 1951 All-Star game. There are plaques commemorating his induction into the

Ohio Hall of Fame, and another recounting his amateur career with Fort Wayne. There are mounted autographed baseballs, and an artist's portrait of him in his Browns uniform. "I got a few things here, I guess," he says, as I examine the photos and plaques.

Garver's career ended ignominiously with the expansion Los Angeles Angels in 1961. Appearing in twelve games, he was winless in three decisions before being released. He is standing in his rec room now, leaning against the fireplace, telling me it wasn't difficult leaving baseball.

"The last few seasons weren't fun anymore. And I never thought I would play forever. So I'd kinda been planning for that. I tried to save a little money. I wanted to be able to get out without being embarrassed. But I made another stupid mistake. Bill DeWitt was down here at Cincinnati, and he called and said, 'We've got a chance to win the pennant, and if you'd go down to Indianapolis and pitch a couple of times and get in shape again, we'll bring you up here, and we think you can help us.' I told Dorothy, 'I don't think they've got a chance to finish better than third.' He laughs. "That was in 1961 and they won the pennant. I might have pitched in the World Series if I had taken his offer."

Instead, he returned home to Ney and farmed with his brother, until taking the public relations job in December 1962.

We have returned to his living room now, and exchange season's greetings at the door as I'm about to depart. Shaking my hand, he returns again to baseball and says, "You know, I enjoyed my time in baseball, but I took it more seriously than I would if I was playing now. I'd smell the roses a little more. I worked year-round at baseball, but I'm proud of what I was able to accomplish." He pauses, releases my hand. "Got some snow coming," he says, indicating the flurries beginning to gather intensity outside. "You be careful on that turnpike."

NED GARVER'S MAJOR LEAGUE CAREER

Year	Team	Games	Won	Lost	ERA
1948	Browns	38	7	11	3.41
1949	Browns	41	12	17	3.98
1950	Browns	37	13	18	3.39
1951	Browns	33	20	12	3.73
1952	Browns	21	7	10	3.68
	Tigers	1	1	0	2.00
1953	Tigers	30	11	11	4.45
1954	Tigers	35	14	11	2.81
1955	Tigers	33	12	16	3.98
1956	Tigers	6	0	2	4.08
1957	Athletics	24	6	13	3.84
1958	Athletics	31	12	11	4.03
1959	Athletics	32	10	13	3.71
1960	Athletics	28	4	9	3.83
1961	Angels	12	0	3	5.59
TOTALS		**402**	**129**	**157**	**3.73**

STAN LOPATA:

Philadelphia Phillies, 1956

"...there were a few ball clubs that used to pull a reverse of the Williams shift on for me, and put the second baseman on the third-base side of the bag. . . . And after I changed my stance I kept hitting line drives and pulling the ball, and it was just one of those fabulous years."

Shortly before I'm about to leave my room at the Ramada Inn in Phoenix to drive a rental car to Mesa, where I'm scheduled to visit ex-Phillies catcher Stan Lopata at his retirement home, my phone rings. It's Lopata telling me I needn't make the drive; he's coming to the airport to pick up his mother-in-law, and it might be more convenient for him to stop by my room in an hour.

I want to talk to him about 1956, the year he set most of the hitting records for a Philadelphia right-handed-batting catcher. That year, only his second as an everyday player, he slugged thirty-two homers and drove in ninety-five runs. He hit thirty-three doubles and seven triples, also team records for catchers. Lopata's major league career spanned 1948 through 1960, and he was named to two National League All-Star teams as a reserve backstop, when Roy Campanella was injured. Yet as a catcher, his principal position, he caught more than a hundred games in only two of those years. During his ten-plus seasons with the Phillies he was mostly a backup to Andy Seminick. He became the starter in 1955 and responded with twenty-two home runs in ninety-nine games, a foretokening of the power potential he would unleash in his banner season of 1956, when his home-run total was sixth-best in the National League.

In 1956 he caught 102 games and divided about forty more between first base and pinch hitting.

But his career went rapidly downhill after 1956, and he again became a utility catcher/first baseman, never hitting more than eighteen homers again in a career that would end after he spent much of the 1960 season in the minors with Louisville.

Lopata is sixty-five when we meet in my hotel room shortly before Christmas. In 1985 he had a quadruple bypass operation, and felt for health reasons he should move to a warmer climate. He moved to a Mesa development called Leisure World in 1986. Prior to the major surgery, he'd been an executive with a Philadelphia concrete company.

He arrives precisely at two o'clock for his appointment. He still carries his weight well, and I doubt he weighs as much as he did during his playing days. Back then he weighed a solid 210 pounds. He's just over six feet two in height, and still seems rawboned-rangy, not in the stereotypical mold of most catchers from his era, who tended to be squat, barrel-chested men. He looks more like a retired first baseman with a 1950s-style crew cut set off by 1970s sideburns of gray-turning-white, which extend to the bottoms of his earlobes.

After we introduce ourselves and make small talk, he settles into the armchair in my room, puts his feet on the footstool, and with a satisfied sigh settles in, his back to the window and the view of Camelback Mountain, shrouded on this warm December afternoon in a sickly yellow-purple carbon dioxide haze against the mountain's sandstone red.

Since he spent most of his final season as a professional ballplayer toiling in the minors, I am curious about why he would agree to be sent down for his swan song.

"Well," he says, stretching and yawning, "I could have played a little longer, and I knew I was past my peak and was gonna retire anyway. John McHale was the general manager at Milwaukee, and he needed my permission to send me down. Milwaukee had a chance of winning the pennant and getting into the World Series, and I said I would lose money. He said, 'Don't worry about it. We'll take care of you.' Which they did. I went down to Louisville and ended up winning the Little World Series, which made me some money, and I also got voted a full share by the Braves, who finished second that year. So in a way I made out better than if I'd stayed in Milwaukee the full season."

We talked awhile about his baseball beginnings. He played high school and American Legion baseball in Detroit, his hometown, but wasn't signed to a pro contract until after his discharge from the service in 1946. "I'd played some semipro ball in 1943 until I was drafted, and then after I got out I played a couple games semipro in Detroit and signed up with the Phillies in 1946, where I started minor league ball in Terre Haute, Indiana. 1947 I went up to Utica and was MVP that year, and we won the championship and the playoffs. We were a Class A league, and a lot of ballplayers on that club went on to the majors. Ashburn played left field for us, and myself, of course, and Granny Hammner. Bill Glenn didn't play much for the Phillies, but he came up with Cleveland. He played first base for us. We had a couple two or three pitchers who had short stays in the big leagues. From there I went to Toronto and from Toronto to Philadelphia in 1948. My first full year with the Phillies was 1949."

His major league baptism was singularly inauspicious. In 1948, he appeared in six games near the end of the season and batted a paltry .133. The next season, as second-string catcher and pinch hitter, he played in eighty-three games and batted a more respectable .271. During the year of the Whiz Kids pennant win, Lopata continued playing behind Andy Seminick, hit .209, and caught one game in the Series, a four-game sweep by the Yankees. He batted only five times in '51, spending most of that year back in the minors.

But his return to the bigs saw him remain as a number-two catcher, this time behind Smoky Burgess. He would not become a regular until 1955, when he was twenty-nine years old. He showed moderate offensive production that year before blossoming as a feared power hitter in 1956.

I ask him about it, and how he happened to hit all those home runs.

A slight smile creases his grizzled face. "Well, most of the time my power was to right center and left center field. That was before I changed my stance. Now everybody credits Hornsby for changing my stance, but he really didn't do it."

Lopata leans forward slightly, coughs, readying himself for the anecdote. "One day we were playing in Chicago and staying at the Edgewater Beach Hotel. Johnny Wyrostek was my roommate, and Rogers Hornsby happened to be in the lobby after we finished breakfast. While I was paying the tab, John went to the lobby, and he knew Rogers Hornsby. They were talking in the lobby and I was coming out, and at the time I wasn't going too well. Johnny said to Hornsby, 'Well, what do you think about this guy?'

"Hornsby looked at me, and he recognized me, and he said, 'I haven't seen him play in person, only on television. But he misses too many balls when he swings the bat. Every time you swing the bat you should hit a piece of the ball. Not necessarily get base hits, but get a piece of the ball.' He didn't mention nothin' about changing my stance, but that day I went out, and I remembered a guy I knew when I was a kid who'd played minor league ball for the Yankees, and he had an open stance, facing the pitcher. He didn't crouch as much as I did, though. So I opened up and I crouched down a little bit and saw the ball real well. That day I got two hits. Next day I came out again and I got down a little lower and I got two or three more hits. So the next day, the third day, we went to Milwaukee, and I got down where I ended up with that stance, real low, and I stayed with it ever since. When I did change my stance I couldn't hit a ball to the right-hand side of the field. Even if I tried to drive a runner over to second, I couldn't do it. No way."

He chuckles. "Matter of fact, there were a few ball clubs that used to pull a reverse of the Williams shift on for me, and put the second baseman on the third-base side of the bag. But I couldn't hit a ball to right field to save my soul. And after I changed my stance I kept hitting line drives and pulling the ball, and it was just one of those fabulous years." He drops his feet to the floor; his voice grows more animated. "It seemed like when the ball was maybe a foot, two feet, out of the pitchers' hands I could tell what was coming by the spin of the ball, whether it was a breaking ball or a fastball, offspeed, whatever." He smacks his hands together. "I just hit everything hard."

He leans back again, feet back on the footstool. I fiddle with the tape recorder to eliminate a hum. Glancing up, I notice the cloud has thickened around Camelback, and voices emanating from the parking lot below say there's another pollution alert today.

But Lopata, a heart-attack victim, the sort of person for whom such an alert would have bearing, seems oblivious. Once again it's 1956, and he's the home-run king in Philadelphia. "Sometimes you see guys like Bo Jackson hit batting practice, and everybody comes over to watch him. Our players used to come out and watch me hit batting practice. It was like hitting a golf ball. I had just a nice and easy stroke."

How does that happen? I ask. How does he account for it?

He chuckles briefly. "If you could account for it, there'd be a lot more .300 hitters. I don't know why I lost it. Maybe it was because I got hit in the head a couple times. Maybe I was careless, maybe I didn't concentrate on the pitchers that much. But if you could find out the reason for it, there'd be guys hittin' .350 or .400. It was just one of those things. It came to me in 1956. Sort of like a gift, I guess you could say."

He smiles, readjusts his position in the chair, declines my offer of coffee, glances at his watch. He's supposed to pick up his mother-in-law in thirty minutes.

I ask him if he thought he'd set a standard for himself in 1956, and whether he thought he'd at least approximate his offensive production in future seasons.

He nods, slumping in the chair. "I thought I was going to continue to have great years like that. But near the end of '56 I got hit in the head, and after that . . ." He shrugs, sighs. "I don't know, maybe it was that or maybe I just lost concentration."

He speaks of his beanings matter-of-factly, without rancor. I ask who was pitching when he was skulled.

Sitting forward, animated again, he tells me that the Phillies were playing the Giants the first time. "Windy McCall was the pitcher. It was toward the end of the year when he hit me in the head. They tell you when you get hit in the head you're supposed to take it easy and get a good night's rest and stuff like that. But this was a night game, and I got to bed maybe one, two o'clock in the morning, and I got up at eight to go to church, and then I played that afternoon—Sunday.

"In the first inning I came up to bat and Reuben Gomez was pitching. He had one of the best curveballs in the game, and I told myself I would just not give in. I would stay in there. I hung right in there and hit the ball out of the ballpark. It was a real good curveball, and when I rounded the bases and got back to the dugout, I keeled over and they took me to the hospital, where they kept me for three days. That was over the Labor Day weekend.

"Now the second time I was hit, it was Larry Jackson in St. Louis." He shrugs. "After home runs, you were always looking for the knockdown pitch. It was part of baseball."

He says the beanings may have affected his batting prowess during the remainder of this career, but refuses to blame those incidents for his decline. "Sure, unconsciously, they might have affected me, but I wasn't aware of it. On the other hand, I've accepted the fact that 1956 may have been just one of those years, because I could do no wrong. It was just a great year."

I mention that some former ballplayers I've talked to have said that after coming off great seasons and falling into prolonged slumps, coaches and managers were all too eager to tamper with the players' mechanics, which sometimes caused players to lose confidence and finally major league skills. Did this happen with him?

He shrugs. "I can see where you *can* get overcoached," he says. "But nowadays, they'll get that camera on a guy when he's going good and when he's going bad, and show him both ways. I think that's good. But a player isn't a piece of machinery. I used to catch against Stan Musial, and when he was in a slump I'd notice that when the ball was a little bit inside or outside, he would swing at it. Not a bad pitch, maybe a half inch off the plate. He'd swing at it and hope maybe he could get back in the groove again. When he's going good, forget it. He'll take it for a ball."

An interesting digression, but I return to my original question and ask again if he thought coaches interfered with him from 1957 to the end of his career, trying to help him recapture his home-run stoke.

"No." His answer is emphatic. "After I got traded by the Phillies I didn't play too much." He frowns slightly, glances at his watch again, and I'm thinking that our interview is about over. He doesn't move, however, but brings his hand to his forehead and rubs it absently. "Another thing about '56," he says. "I hurt my knee. We were playing Cincinnati and I was working out, and the trainer said there was nothing wrong with the knee. I couldn't run, I couldn't catch, but they said I could play. Well, in those days you really couldn't argue with the bosses, so I said I'd try to catch. But Mayo Smith didn't put me in the lineup that day until the ninth inning when we were one run behind. I went up to pinch-hit. Birdie Tebbets, the Cincinnati manager, came out to talk to his pitcher. Seemed like he was out there five minutes. Well, he threw at me." Lopata chuckles briefly. "But after a couple pitches I hit one out of the ballpark. I limped around the bases because I couldn't run. We won the ball game, and that game stands out because I won it, and also because I couldn't run."

Stan Lopata spent nearly all of his big league years in Philadelphia, a city not known to suffer ordinariness from its professional athletes. Did the Phillies' fans and media come to expect more from him than he was capable of delivering after 1956?

His face and voice are expressionless. "The fans treated me pretty good, but I did feel sorry for Del Ennis. He was a real good all-around player, and a lot of people didn't give him the credit he deserved. He hit thirty home runs and about a hundred RBI for about ten years in a row, and he was a local boy, and they used to boo the heck out of him. There were a lot of things the fans didn't know about—personal life. His wife was sick, and fans didn't know about that. And yeah, after a while they got on me too, but it didn't bother me. By then I had six, seven years under my belt. Maybe if it'd been the first or second year it'd have been different.

"They always picked on people, though, and at that time it was Del Ennis, who was making quite a bit of money, and they finally traded him. After I started going bad they got after me. Maybe they thought I should have been having a better year, and . . ." He pauses, shrugs. "I don't know—they had to get after somebody, I guess." He offers a slight smile.

"One thing I'm glad to see, though, is this thing in Philadelphia now, where they took the beer away from the fans. That'll help. 'Cause somebody's gonna get hurt bad. I mean, back then a guy'd get a beer dumped on him, but now they throw batteries and stuff that could really hurt someone."

A question I've always wanted to ask a catcher is whether playing that demanding position shortens a career. So I ask him.

"No, I don't think so. I mean, I quit because I was tired of the traveling. After I quit, Roy Hamey, who was with the Yankees then, wanted me to go down to Richmond to play and coach, but I'd had enough traveling. From 1943, when I went into the service, until 1960, I'd lived out of a suitcase. I was married with seven kids. I just got tired of it. I probably could have stayed around and gotten picked up because they were starting to expand the major leagues about then, but I figured I wanted to get out of it while my name was still in somebody's memory, so I could maybe get a decent job somewhere. And it turned out real well.

"Having a baseball name opened a lot of doors for me, but once a door is open, you still have to deliver."

He stands to leave; our abbreviated interview is over. I walk him to the door and take the elevator down to the lobby with him. He tells me he missed baseball the first couple of years away from it, but is somewhat bored with the game now. "I seldom go out to a ball game anymore, and when I do, along about the fifth or sixth inning, why, that's it. That's enough."

These days he's enjoying his retirement. He plays golf with his wife about four times a week, and has become rather skilled at woodcarving. A doll he crafted sold for $250 at a major league baseball alumni association charity auction.

"Hey," he says, shaking my hand near the hotel's front exit, "good talking to you. Like I said, baseball's been good to me. I did something that I really loved, and got paid for it." He chuckles again. "Hey, you can't beat that, can you?"

STAN LOPATA'S MAJOR LEAGUE CAREER

Year	Team	Games	Home Runs	RBI	BA
1948	Phillies	6	0	2	.133
1949	Phillies	83	8	27	.271
1950	Phillies	58	1	11	.209
1951	Phillies	3	0	0	.000
1952	Phillies	57	4	27	.274
1953	Phillies	81	8	31	.239
1954	Phillies	86	14	42	.290
1955	Phillies	99	22	58	.271
1956	Phillies	146	32	95	.267
1957	Phillies	116	18	67	.237
1958	Phillies	86	9	33	.248
1959	Braves	25	0	4	.104
1960	Braves	7	0	0	.125
TOTALS		**853**	**116**	**397**	**.254**

Bob "Hurricane" Hazle:

Milwaukee Braves, 1957

". . . I said, I won't be sent back, no matter what happens, for not tryin', for not swingin' the bat. . . . I was not gonna go up there and take strikes down the middle of the plate, or take balls and try for walks. I was gonna swing the bat."

In its long history, baseball has given us more than fabled careers and significant seasons. There have also been golden moments forever fixed in our memories. Few who saw them will ever forget Al Gionfrido's catch that robbed Joe DiMaggio of a home run in the 1947 World Series, Willie Mays's stunning over-the-shoulder grab of the Vic Wertz fly in the 1954 series, Don Larsen's 1956 perfect game, Roger Maris's sixty-first home run, and Henry Aaron's home run number 715.

Yet sometimes, stunning performances linger beyond the moment, stretch into days or weeks when the ballplayer is on a roll, when the ball looks like a grapefruit to the batter who can't make an out, when everything he hits finds the hole. A hitter loves those streaks, and when he's going bad, he tries to regroup psychologically, to recapture everything he had when he was hot.

Sometimes it seems to the ballplayer that the streak will go on forever. For two months—August and September 1957—a journeyman outfielder with the Milwaukee Braves swung the hottest bat in the major leagues. Twenty-six-year-old Bob Hazle became a household name during the closing drive for the National League pennant, and would be accorded the dubious accolade by the *Sports Book of Lists* as baseball's biggest flash in the pan. His big league career was notable only during those two months, and one year later he was out of the majors for good.

On a sun-splashed afternoon in late October, my plane lands in Columbia, South Carolina, where Bob Hazle has lived since signing his first professional baseball contract back in 1950. The city, as is the fashion these days, has undergone wholesale gentrification. Its main streets are wide and tree-lined, and its trendy restaurants and boutiques feature the obligatory plethora of ferns and dieffenbachia. There's a sterile beauty here that is not altogether unpleasant, but save the presence of a line of palm trees in front of a downtown bank, one might just as easily be in Rockford, Illinois, as in the cradle of the old South.

Hazle acknowledges that he's merely a baseball trivia figure these days, but doesn't worry about it. He says it gives him a continuing notoriety more than thirty years after he played his last game in the major leagues.

In all, Hazle would play in only 110 big league games in an abbreviated career that spanned parts of just three seasons. Though his lifetime batting average was a lusty .310, that average was bolstered by the blistering .403 he batted during the final two months of the 1957 season with the World Series Champion Milwaukee Braves.

Called up by the Braves on July 28 following an injury to Billy Bruton, Hazle entered the starting lineup on August 4 with the Braves trailing the Cardinals by a game. In his first game against the Dodgers, Hazle hit a single and a double and scored a run in the Braves' 9–7 win. His torrid hitting led the Braves to ten straight wins, which broke the backs of St. Louis and Brooklyn and put Milwaukee in front to stay.

Leading the Cardinals by two and a half games on August 9, Milwaukee went into St. Louis for a three-game series. In the first game, Hazle hit three singles and a home run, scored a run, and drove in two more, pacing the 13–2 win. In the series he went seven for ten, drove in four runs, and scored three times. In that ten-game winning streak, Hazle batted .545, with eighteen hits in thirty-three at bats, driving in eleven runs.

But he never really cooled off at all during the pennant drive. His on-base percentage was .477, and his .629 slugging average was slightly higher than that of the league leader, Willie Mays. That two-month span in 1957 was an authentic *Field of Dreams* for Hazle, with hit after hit continuing to drop. He made thirty-four hits in his first sixty-seven at bats by August 30, prompting teammate Red Schoendienst to say, "Right now the kid is Stan Musial, Mickey Mantle, and Ted Williams all wrapped in one." And outfielder Andy Pafko, with whom the left-handed-hitting Hazle was platooned, said, "Next to Hank Aaron, he's got the strongest wrists in baseball." Hazle finished the year with fifty-four hits in 134 at bats. Though he would get only two hits in thirteen times at bat during the World Series, 1957 was a storybook season for the journeyman ballplayer who almost quit the game at the end of 1956.

Bob Hazle meets me at the airport in his white 1982 Buick Riviera. At fifty-eight, he is a handsome, square-jawed man with a full head of gray hair. He is wearing a blue windbreaker, yellow polo shirt, and gray slacks. He appears slightly shorter than his listed playing height of six feet, but weighs only two pounds more than his playing weight of 190. His weight, though, he tells me later, is too much. He suffered two massive heart attacks in 1982, resulting in triple bypass surgery, and likes to keep himself around 185 these days. He also walks with a very slight limp. His oft-injured left knee has been bothering him lately, and he's considering surgery. "I'd like to be able to play a little more golf," he tells me, "and if you want to know the truth, I'd like to be able to trot. I go to these old-timers' games, and I can't believe how bad I look out there. Now if I could at least trot, that wouldn't be so bad."

Originally signed by Cincinnati after graduating from high school in Woodruff, South Carolina, in 1950, Hazle spent his rookie year playing here in the old Class A Sally League. Since leaving the game after the 1960 season, spent with Little Rock in the Double A Southern Association, he's made his living in sales—real estate, insurance, tombstones. For the last few years, he's represented a large wholesale liquor distributor in Columbia.

He is warm, cordial in the manner of many native Southerners. We discuss the weather, which has been unseasonably cool hereabouts.

Bob Hazle lives just outside the city limits in a large rambler on Dorset Drive. Inside, we sit in the den just off the kitchen overlooking the backyard pool and Jacuzzi. Mementoes of his baseball career dominate his den. On the wall above his desk is a pencil drawing of him in his Milwaukee uniform, a gift from a fan. Next to it is a certificate commemorating his induction into the Woodruff Hall of Fame. A standout high school athlete, Hazle was all-state in football, basketball, and baseball, earning sixteen letters in these sports, plus tennis. A Silver Glove for being the best defensive left fielder in the American Association with Charleston, West Virginia, in 1959 is on his desk, and remains a valued trophy. "The rap against me in the big leagues was that I couldn't field," he says.

On the mantel above the fireplace are commemorative mugs celebrating the Braves' World Series win, another from the Indianapolis Indians, with whom he toiled in 1954, and a baseball autographed by his Tiger teammates in 1958. "I got about a dozen autographed balls," he tells me. "I rotate 'em up here every now and then. I got one from Milwaukee, and some are from the minor leagues and a couple all-star teams I made in the minors." There's also the Milwaukee Rookie of the Year plaque, awarded him after the 1957 season.

He apologizes for the clutter in the house, clearing space on a table for my tape recorder and notebook amid stacks of mail, much of it requests for autographs, which he dutifully signs and returns. Autograph requests don't bother him, he says, smiling. "Tell the truth, it would bother me more if it stopped."

I ask him to tell me the story he's told to dozens of reporters and writers over the years, to tell me about his meteoric major league career, which shone brilliantly in August and September 1957, then plummeted with equal velocity the following year.

He nods, folds his hands. "Well now, it was just wonderful," he says quietly. "Just wonderful. You're talkin' '57 now, right? See, the reason I got called up in the first place was because Bruton broke his leg. Milwaukee was wanting a left-handed-hitting outfielder. So they were trying to decide who to bring up, or if they wanted to make a trade for another outfielder. Ben Geraghty was the one who had a lot to do with me being called up. He was the manager at Wichita, where I was playin' at the time. At the beginning of the season there, and for a long time, I was discouraged and I halfway didn't care, if I haveta put it that way."

He'd spent the previous year in Wichita, and had made the all-star team. He was disappointed when the Braves didn't invite him to spring training. "I talked it over with my wife, and I said, 'Well, this is it. I'll try it one more year and if it doesn't work out, I'll quit baseball.' Tell you the truth, I had to work to keep the old adrenaline flowing, 'cause sure, I was discouraged.

"Anyway, I was hittin' about .216 most of the season. They had another outfielder there hitting good, Ray Shearer, who was a right-handed hitter, and he was hitting a lot higher than I was and had a lot more home runs. I figured if they were gonna call up anybody, it would have been him. But they wanted a left-handed hitter, and I'd been on a streak." In just a few weeks, he'd raised his average more than 60 points to .279.

"I was in Denver that morning at breakfast when they told me I was going up—get my clothes packed, that I was going to Milwaukee. Ben Geraghty told them to take me because I was the hottest hitter they had going at the time. I was always a streak hitter, and he told them, why not use me while I was hot."

At the time of his call-up by the Braves, Hazle had also hit twelve home runs and driven in fifty-nine runs in 102 games at Wichita.

"It was a real good feeling to be lucky enough to be called up by Milwaukee, because a lot of good Triple A ballplayers never got a shot. I thought it was a lucky break for me."

While he'd been hitting well during the last weeks at Wichita, he would be even hotter in the majors. Why was that?

He chuckles. "If I knew, I'd tell you. When I got there, though, I said, I won't be sent back, no matter what happens, for not tryin', for not swingin' the bat. What I meant was, I was not gonna go up there and take strikes down the middle of the plate, or take balls and try for walks. I was gonna swing the bat. And if the hits came, they came. I wasn't gonna be called out on third strikes or things like that. If I was sent back it was gonna be because I couldn't hit, or what-have-you. And the hits came."

Did they ever. He grins when I read him the Red Schoendienst quote.

"What can I say—that made me feel real good. It just made me feel good to go up and help the team. That's what I wanted to do. It would have been nice if I'd been all those things—Ted Williams and all—and I'd have played longer. That's really my only regret, that I couldn't have played longer in the big leagues. It would have been nice to get a pension. But that's life."

He's interrupted by a phone call from his wife, Pat, whom he calls Mama. We're to pick her up from work at six. This is the second marriage for both Bob and Pat. The first Mrs. Hazle died in 1970.

Though Hurricane Hazle's career was a brief one in the big leagues, he's acquired more press clippings than many who played upward of five to ten years. He was the center of much media attention in Milwaukee, often getting more ink than future Hall-of-Famers Henry Aaron, Eddie Matthews, and Warren Spahn. How, I wonder, did he cope with that—going from obscurity in the minors to celebrity status in the big leagues within weeks?

"It was great, and I enjoyed it. Golly, I couldn't go out for steak without somebody picking up the tab. The milkman delivered milk and there was no charge. I mean, you couldn't walk into a club but somebody's buyin' your drinks. Now the press was always askin' me why things were goin' so good, and like I said earlier, I can't answer that. I told 'em I swung the bat. It felt good to get the publicity, but my gosh, it wasn't just me. We had a good team that year. Good ballplayers, good leadership. We stuck together and played together and pulled for each other. I like to think I helped."

That Bob Hazle merely helped was, of course, an understatement. He refers to a crucial game against the Phillies in Philadelphia, won by the Braves 7–1. Hazle leans forward over the table, a grin creasing his face. "In that game I had three out of four. Two of 'em was home runs, and each home run I had two men on base, so I drove in six runs that day. The other run came when Warren Spahn hit a home run."

He laughs, shakes his head. "Eddie Matthews still kids me about that game. On that day a gale was blowin' in from right field. Now, I'm a left-handed batter, and Eddie, as you remember, could hit the ball an awful long ways. Now, he says he's trying to hit the ball to left, and here comes Hazle hitting into right field against that gale. Right out of the park. Then Hazle comes up again and hits one over the scoreboard in right center against that wind. Yeah, I guess that was one of my best hitting days." He pauses, reflecting on the moment he's relived endlessly over the passing of more than thirty years, the shining moment in a shining streak that ended all too soon.

He starts in again now, relishing the retelling of his phenomenal prowess in 1957. "I was usually battin' seventh," he says. "I think it was Logan leading off, Schoendienst hittin' second, Matthews third, Aaron fourth, and Joe Adcock would be fifth, and then, of course, Wes Covington sixth, and I'm seventh. I imagine maybe the pitchers let up on me because after they got through Aaron and Matthews, they may have unconsciously eased off. Then—*whew*—they could let up a little bit, you know?"

He sits up in his chair and pantomimes a swing with the bat. "I didn't have the reputation as a power hitter or anything like that. In the minors, like anyone else, I was always struggling to hit. I mean, I always thought I *could* hit, but I wasn't cocky. If you don't believe in yourself, you might as well forget it. But sometimes a pitcher would get me out easy, and sometimes he didn't. My pitch was an inside fastball knee-high. You don't pitch me that inside fastball," he says, standing, taking his stance, eyeing an imaginary pitch knee-high, swinging, and driving it deep to right field.

He sits, laughs again. "I probably remember every one of my hits in the major leagues. I remember in Chicago—and at this time I did not have my family with me in Milwaukee. I talked to John Quinn [Milwaukee general manager] about it and he said, 'Pick up the phone, call 'em and have 'em here tonight.' Well, I called the family and they flew in the next day. I had a friend meet 'em at the airport and bring 'em to the game. I had two for four that day. It was tied seven–seven in the eighth or ninth inning. I hit a home run to make it eight–seven, and we won the game. And my family was there to see that."

He pauses, reflecting again, a slight smile creasing his lips. I glance at my watch and tell him it will soon be six o'clock, time to pick up Pat. "Well, we seem to be on a roll here," he says. "It's not that important that we be there right at six. It'll be okay."

I ask what he remembers most clearly about clinching the National League pennant in 1957.

Still smiling, he nods. "We clinched it in Milwaukee against St. Louis. Aaron homered to win the game. Now, I wasn't playin' in that game. I thought I might get to pinch-hit, but I didn't. Well, we all went to the Wisconsin Club after the game, and believe me, there were twenty-five ballplayers who didn't want to play ball the next day." He laughs heartily. "Oooh, boy, but this was something. I never dreamed I'd be in a World Series. It was a wonderful break to get to Milwaukee in the first place, and now I'm going to be in the Series. Words can't describe it. You felt great. I was just floating. This was the ultimate in baseball, to win the World Series. There's a lot of players who play in the major leagues fifteen years and never make the Series. Here I am, a scrubini, and get to play in one and get a World Series ring." He shows it to me, places the heavy adornment in my palm. It's evident this is his prized possession, a memento that still defines Bob Hazle, ballplayer.

Though the Braves defeated the Yankees in seven games behind Lew Burdette's three victories, Hazle managed only two hits in thirteen at bats during the classic—perhaps a foretokening of what was to follow in 1958. That year would be his swan song in the big leagues, and he wouldn't even finish it in Milwaukee, where only months earlier hundreds of beer steins were raised and toasts honoring his name were on the lips of the rabid Braves fans.

What about 1958? I want to know. What caused the collapse of the dream and the career?

He offers a shrug and a sigh. "I started hitting okay that spring, but instead of being real loose, I guess I started being a little more cautious. It's hard to stay calm, but in 1957 I was really loose. I had nothing to lose in '57. Now in '58, I'm wantin' to be up there for years, and I might have tightened up a little bit. But I still felt good. I was hitting all right. Then in an exhibition game, Tom Morgan hit me in the head. He didn't mean to, it was just one of those things. Then in a game against Pittsburgh, Whammy Douglas hit me in the back. I think I slid into second base in a game in Chicago, and hurt my ankle a little bit. I came out and went back in the lineup later. Then in St. Louis I hit real good. I got about three for four and drove in four runs. Hit good. Now it's the third game of the series, and we jumped off and got five runs in the first inning. I came up and Covington had just hit a home run in front of me to bring in Frank Torre. I'm standin' at the plate, and Frank says, 'Don't dig in.' I says, 'You know I won't.' They changed pitchers then and Larry Jackson came in.

"They stood on the mound talkin' after he took his warm-up pitches. You can about picture what I did in the batter's box." Hazle is up now, demonstrating, drawing an imaginary plate on the floor of the den, standing well back in the box. "Jackson started his windup, and when he got about head-high with his pitch, I just stepped back, sort of backed out of the box. I'm just givin' him his pitch, you know? I'm just backin' up—and the pitch was behind me. And so I'd already started my motion. If I hadn't started my motion I'd have been all right. I tried to drop out of the way of it, and I threw up my hand to block it." He is leaning back, demonstrating his attempt to evade the pitch. "But it came through and hit me on the ear. I was about three feet out of the batter's box. Only thing I remember was Eddie Matthews being held back. He was after somebody. That's about the last I remember. I was floating. I stayed in the hospital there for two weeks while the team flew on to San Francisco.

"My equilibrium was off. I'd look up and get dizzy. Same thing when I looked down. Then I went back to Milwaukee and started workin' out while the team was still on the road. Billy Bruton was coming back from a heel injury, and he and I would work out together. Just runnin' and trying to get my equilibrium back. Finally, I'm okay, and I played one game against Cincinnati. I got one for three, drove in a run, and we went back to Milwaukee. I was on the bench waitin' to see who was in the startin' lineup and Fred Haney walked down the bench and said I was sold to Detroit."

There's a trace of bitterness in his voice when he relates this. "They don't ask you. They look at your teeth, they feel of your leg—you're just like a racehorse, and they say, 'Trade him.' My bottom fell out. I didn't want to leave the team. I thought that team was gonna be a good team and I felt I would help, even though in '58 my hitting wasn't that great." The fact was, after playing in twenty games, the old Hurricane wasn't hitting his weight. He'd managed only ten hits in fifty-six at bats, none of them home runs, and his average was an anemic .179.

"I was a streak hitter," he explains. It's important for him to explain. He never got a chance to argue his case before John Quinn. "Who's to say I wouldn't get another one going again? So over to Detroit I go, and naturally it didn't make me feel good, but yet I'm in the majors and I'm gonna make the best of it. Jack Tighe is the manager there, and he's a good fella. I liked him. When I get there—only thing I can tell you is I was just another outfielder. They had about a dozen of them. What they wanted with me I don't know. So with Detroit I played a game every now and then. I thought I hit pretty well. Then I was on the bench again after they fired Jack Tighe and brought in Bill Norman. He decided to go with the old lineup, and I only got to play a ball game once in a while. I worked out, tried to keep my spirits up, but it's hard to do when you don't get your chance. You don't get the chance to show, and then when you pinch-hit or something— it's hard, that's all." He shakes his head. "Any player will tell you this; it's hard to come up cold off the bench. Certain ones are gifted at it—Dusty Rhodes, Smoky Burgess, guys like that. And it's hard to keep your attitude up. As the year went on it got rougher. I got discouraged about not playin', just sittin' and gettin' the RA. You know what RA is, don't you? That's the red ass.

"Anyway, at the end of the year Detroit wanted to trade me, but other teams would say I was hurt, I couldn't play. Nobody ever asked me. So when they don't believe in you, you don't have a chance, and they sent me to Triple A."

There's a long pause. Bob Hazle is gazing outside, beyond his pool, beyond his backyard. The only sound for several long moments is the whispery whir of my tape recorder.

Finally he looks over at me. "When you're down in Triple A—how can I say it—it's just hard to get the adrenaline flowin' again, when you felt like you wasn't gonna get a shot anyway."

He looks down at the tape recorder and sighs. "That's life, and maybe if I could have shook it and given it my best shot, it'd have been different. Who knows what could have happened to me? Don't misunderstand—but the parks are not the same in Triple A, towns are not the same. When you've been up there, got used to that big league livin', people recognizin' you, sometimes you get disheartened [returning to the minors]. I couldn't get the adrenaline going playing at Charleston, West Virginia."

In his last hurrah, Hazle finished the 1958 season by hitting .241 in fifty-eight at bats with the Tigers. He appeared in forty-three games, struck two home runs, and drove in five runs.

It's nearly six-thirty when the phone rings. It's his wife, who tells him she's secured a ride home and we needn't bother interrupting the interview.

"Sorry about that," he says, returning to the table. "Now where were we? 1959? Yeah. After that year at Charleston I was disgusted. I came back home. They wanted me to go to Birmingham in the Southern Association, which was Double A. I talked to the wife and I said, 'This is it. I'm through.'"

But dreams die hard, and for a man who's experienced adulation in the major leagues, the dreams persist, insinuating themselves into the conscious and unconscious mind, consuming the athlete. His dreams of baseball success are his self-identity, his *raison d'être*. And he cannot let go of them, even years after his career is over. In Bob Hazle's case, he was still a young man, only twenty-eight years old in 1960. So he went to spring training.

"Fred Hatfield was the manager over at Little Rock, and he said, 'Bob, I got some old-timers over here, and I'd like to have you join us and have some fun. I'm gonna buy you.' I said, 'Suits me, Fred. But I can tell you right now, when I come over there, that's it. I'm through with baseball end of this year.'

"Well, they had Bob Thorp, who'd been up in the majors, and Eric Roden too. Fred said we'd have some fun, so that's what I did, and at the end of the year, that was it. After that year I was through, and it didn't matter who called or anything. I knew I was quitting, even though I really felt at the time I could have played. But I couldn't play under those conditions."

With that he excuses himself and returns moments later with his old Braves road uniform. It's neatly pressed, on a hanger. "This is the uniform I wore in the Series," he says, handing it to me. I'm surprised at the heaviness of it. The uniform was a thick wool fabric, and even the long-sleeved sweatshirt was wool. "I never really got used to that wool against my skin," he says, handing me his old Braves warm-up jacket. "This is worth nine hundred dollars right now."

He returns the uniform to a closet and produces two thirty-four-inch cordovan-colored Louisville Sluggers. "These are the bats I used in the Series," he says. "I got hats from all the rest of the teams I played on too."

His wife, Pat, enters then, a slim, attractive woman with gray hair. She suggests we go out to dinner, and can continue talking if necessary. We drive a short distance to the 7 Oaks Shopping Mall, and a Greek restaurant, Zorba's.

Pat tells me she met Bob years after his playing career ended, but has taken a genuine interest in the attention he continues to receive from old fans and the media. "Honey, when we get back, you play that Earl Gillespie record for Michael," she says.

Upon our return, she puts a long-playing record on the phonograph and takes out an envelope of recent newspaper and magazine pieces on Bob. "This record," she says, "is highlights from 1957." Then the voice of the Braves, Earl Gillespie, crackles over the stereo speakers: ". . . a fly ball to deep right center field, is a home run for Bob Hazle." Moments later Gillespie is saying, "Again a high fly ball—over the scoreboard in right field. Hazle's driven in six runs today." The record jumps ahead to the Chicago game Bob earlier described to me. "There's a drive to right field. Going back is Walt Moryn, and it's a home run. The Braves lead eight to seven."

"I don't know if that's gonna do him any good, Mama," Bob protests weakly. "He isn't interested in that."

"Of course he is," Pat answers. "You don't know what will be useful to a writer."

Sometimes, I tell her, a writer doesn't know either, but he appreciates the opportunity to get his hands on as much material as possible.

Our formal interview has ended. But I want to know how he got the nickname Hurricane.

He chuckles. "I'll tell you what—if some ballplayer comes along next couple years and his name is Hugo, you better believe he's gonna be called Hurricane too. Now, in 1954 there was a hurricane named Hazel, hit Myrtle Beach. First time I heard anyone call me Hurricane was in 1954. After the season I went down to Maracaibo, Venezuela, to play winter ball. I'm introduced to the owner of the team I'm gonna play for, who cannot speak English, and I cannot speak Spanish. Well, this owner, he

looked at me and he looked back at the interpreter and starts"—
here Hazle makes a whooshing noise, puffing his cheeks—"blowing,
you know, like a hurricane. I been Hurricane ever since. Had
nothin' to do with baseball."

Before we retire for the night, he offers to drive me to the
airport next morning to catch a six-o'clock flight.

When I come into the kitchen at five, he hands me a cup of
coffee. "You'll have to pardon it," he says. "This is what my dad
always called 'sudden' coffee. It's instant."

We sit in the predawn silence and sip coffee. For some reason
I mention current players' salaries compared to money earned
when he played. "I'll tell you something," he says, suddenly alert.
"When I was goin' good there in '57, everybody said I should get
a better contract. I was gettin' somewhere around the minimum.
All the guys told me to go and see Mr. Quinn. Which I did. He
told me that he'd take care of me at the end of the season with a
sort of bonus. I believed him. But when I got the check, it was so
small, my pride wouldn't let me accept it, and I sent it back."
Though he doesn't mention the amount, according to an earlier
magazine story it was only $1,000.

Yet his memories of Milwaukee and the pennant race of 1957
are evergreen. Just before we leave for the airport, we are
walking across his leaf-covered front lawn, and he tells me he
regularly runs into a number of former major leaguers who make
their homes in South Carolina. He mentions Don Buddin,
Johnny Temple, John Buzhardt, Neil Chrisley, and Ty Cline. "We
try to get together now and again to play a little golf."

As the Hurricane unlocks his car, he looks over at me and
pauses. "You know," he says, speaking softly, turning his face
toward the north, "one thing I really would enjoy would be
gettin' invited back to Milwaukee for an old-timers' game. I've
been to Atlanta, and was at an autograph show in Milwaukee last
year, but what I'd really like to do would be to put the uniform
on and step out on that field there one more time."

BOB HAZLE'S MAJOR LEAGUE CAREER

Year	Team	Games	Home Runs	RBI	BA
1955	Reds	6	0	0	.231*
1957	Braves	41	7	27	.403
1958	Braves	20	0	5	.179
	Tigers	43	2	5	.241
TOTALS		**110**	**9**	**37**	**.310**

LEE THOMAS:

Los Angeles Angels, 1962

"One time I got nine hits in a doubleheader . . . and the ball looked like a basketball. . . . I could pick up the ball out of the pitcher's hand, and it seemed like I could almost stop the ball."

When I arrive at Veterans Stadium on Broad Street in Philadelphia, I don't know the location of the Phillies' offices, where I have an appointment with Lee Thomas, the ball club's newly named general manager. Thomas, one of only a handful of ex-players to hold top management positions in baseball, enjoyed a particularly successful season in 1962 as first baseman for the two-year-old Los Angeles Angels franchise. That year Thomas batted .290, slugged twenty-six home runs, and knocked in 104 runs.

But I find myself lost and floundering in the basement bowels of the stadium, in the process dropping and losing an expensive scarf. Finally I'm directed to an elevator and take it to the fourth floor, where the ambience surrounding the cheerful receptionist might be best described as latent Steve Carlton. His old uniform is prominently displayed in a glass case, along with his four Cy

Young Awards. Sharing space in the Carlton exhibit were Cy Young Awards earned by other Phillies pitchers John Denny and Steve Bedrosian. Soft rock music emanates from the receptionist's radio, and front-office employees walk briskly through the area, greeting visitors and sales representatives. There's a business atmosphere here, and no baseball terminology can be discerned through the dim buzz of distant conversations. I could just as easily be in the waiting room of any generic corporation. I remind myself that there's no reason why it should be different. Baseball *is* a business—and a profitable one at that.

After perhaps ten minutes, I'm ushered into Thomas's spacious office, where the Phillies' general manager, wearing a gray suit, white shirt, and patterned maroon tie, sits in a stuffed swivel chair behind a large mahogany desk, the top of which is suitably cluttered. There's a floor-to-ceiling bookcase to his left, containing what appear to be stacks of scouting reports. Facing Thomas on the wall before him are rosters listing all the personnel on every major league team, the names highlighted in red, blue, green, and yellow, which must, I'm thinking, be of some significance. However, I will forget to ask him about the color designations.

A fresh copy of this morning's *Philadelphia Inquirer* is on the floor next to his desk, and in front of the desk and slightly to the left is a VCR next to a stone-dead dieffenbachia gone limp and autumn-brown.

A native of Peoria, Illinois, Lee Thomas is a handsome man who, despite graying hair thinning at the crown, appears younger than his fifty-three years. He was a sturdy six feet two, 195 pounds during his playing days, and his weight seems not to have fluctuated much since his major league career ended in 1968.

He is polite and somewhat formal as we get underway, and he

asks if I'd like coffee, which he fetches himself. Then, leaning back in his chair, he asks, "So what is it you'd like to know?"

I turn on my recorder and ask him to tell me about 1962.

"Well, I always wanted to play with the Yankees," he begins. "I thought I *would* play with the Yankees, because they signed me and I was in their chain seven and a half years. I made the ball club in 1961, but never had a chance to play, and was traded over to Los Angeles." The expansion Angels were mostly composed of cast-offs from other American League teams, and weren't expected to do much. They finished eighth in the ten-team league that year, but distinguished themselves offensively by having five players hit twenty or more home runs. Thomas, a twenty-five-year-old rookie, swatted twenty-four and drove in seventy runs. "That year, and for a few years after, I always seemed to do pretty well against the Yankees. I wanted to prove to them, I suppose, that they'd made a mistake. So anyway, '62 was our first year in Dodger Stadium. We played in the Coliseum in 1961. Dodger Stadium was a pitchers' park then. I think the power alleys have been moved in ten or fifteen feet since then. But '62 was an interesting season. You might remember we were only one and a half games out in September. We just had a lot of fun. We were loose. We were a bunch of guys that nobody wanted. So we surprised a lot of people. We were happy-go-lucky and enjoyed ourselves. I liked Bill Rigney, the manager. If you couldn't play for Rigney, you couldn't play anyplace. He was a tough manager for pitchers, but was great to the everyday guys."

We were interrupted for the first of more than a half-dozen times during the hour by a phone call. It appears to be about a real estate deal, not baseball. He is forceful with the caller, and proposes contacting an attorney. After several minutes he completes the call and returns to 1962.

"Let's see—we were playing the Yankees in September at Yankee Stadium, and I think we were a game and a half out of first. We had a five-game series with them. Well, we lose the first game, then we win the next two. I remember hitting a two- or three-run homer off Whitey Ford. You didn't get too many base hits off him, but this homer won the game for us in the eighth or ninth inning. Then the fourth game was really the turning point for us. We got into the eighth inning with a four-run lead. And we're in first place if we win this game. But the Yankees came back to score five or six runs in the bottom of the ninth to beat us. They proceeded to beat us the next game. Then the Yankees went to Baltimore and we went home. They lost five in a row at Baltimore and we lost five in a row at home. That shows you what could have happened that year. From then on, I think, we ended up third." The Angels faded badly in the stretch, finishing behind the Yankees and Twins, ten games back, and only a half-game in front of fourth-place Detroit. He frowns and exhales. "It was all downhill after that. Here we were, a bunch of ragtag guys who really had a chance to win it all." He frowns, shrugs.

I ask him to describe his personal achievements in 1962.

"Well, I'd come off a pretty good year in 1961, and I had a lot of confidence in my ability to be a decent hitter in the big leagues. Confidence had something to do with it, because there's certainly a mental aspect to hitting. I know when I was going good, I could pick up the ball out of the pitcher's hand, and it seemed like I could almost stop the ball. It looked like a grapefruit when I was going well. Of course, when I was in a slump it looked like a golf ball. One time I got nine hits in a doubleheader, which tied a major league record, and the ball looked like a basketball." He grins.

"We scored a lot of runs in 1962, and I just thought that if men were on base, I should be able to drive them in. Again, it's a confidence thing. I'd always hit with pretty good power in the minors, and drove in a lot of runs. So my success after I got to the big leagues didn't really surprise me. I thought I'd get to the big leagues sooner than I did, and I suppose if I'd had it to do all over again I wouldn't sign with the Yankees, because you could get buried in that organization. I mean, I don't think three and a half years with one minor league ball club is typical. I spent three and a half years at Binghamton in Class A ball. I had good seasons too, hit over twenty home runs two or three times, a hundred RBIs. But as you recall, the Yankees were powers then. If I'd been with some other organization I think I might have gotten to the big leagues a year or two earlier."

Players from the pre–World War II era often made careers playing in the minor leagues. Postwar players were not so inclined, and neither were major league teams likely to keep a player for more than a few seasons if it didn't appear that player would make it to the majors. Thomas, however, toiled more than seven seasons in the minors before getting his shot at the big time. I'm curious about this and wonder if he ever thought of giving up during that lengthy minor league apprenticeship.

"Yes, there were lots of times when I considered giving it up," he said, and offers a half-chuckle. "But I kept saying I've put this much time into it, and what am I gonna do—drive a truck or get some other type job? I just decided to stick with it."

At this point, William Giles, president of the Phillies, comes in, casually dressed in slacks and a dark blue sweater. Thomas introduces us, addressing Giles as "Mr. Giles." Giles produces a newspaper clip and shows it to Thomas. Both men laugh. They chat for a few minutes, before President Giles smiles and exits. "Now where were we?" Thomas says. "Sorry."

I ask him whether his playing days, and especially 1962, left him with vivid impressions. Did he think this season would be his best ever?

"I didn't know," he says. "I thought my average was probably a bit high for me. I was up around .300 there. But I don't remember everything, because as you go through a season, you don't think it will necessarily be more important than another season. When I run across Bill Rigney or Jim Fregosi, or other guys from that team, we'll start to reminisce and some of it comes back to you pretty clear. It was probably the most exciting year for me as a player. And I can remember when I got a base hit that won a game, or hit a home run. I also remember when I got an error or struck out to lose a ball game. I remember certain times in the year when people thought we were going to be folding, and we kept winning. I can remember the ballparks we played in like it was yesterday."

Also vivid in his mind was the injury to his knee. "About midyear in '62 I tore the cartilage in my knee, and there was talk about me quitting and having operation. I'd just gotten off to such a good start I said to heck with it. I'm gonna go ahead and play. And I did. I played the last half of the season on torn cartilage and I ended up having the kind of year I needed to have and wanted to have. Then I had the operation during the winter. And in 1963, you know, well, there's just no excuses. I stunk up the joint. Rigney gave me every opportunity. Hell, I got to bat five hundred times. I was just horrible." He scowls, shakes his head in disgust.

"When I look back on '63 it was probably the most frustrating year in baseball that I've spent as a player. No matter what I tried to do I just got myself in deeper. I had somewhat of a temper then, and it was probably easier for other guys to get out of a slump than it was for me. Here I was off back-to-back pretty good years in the big leagues and I said I know this can't happen to me, and sooner or later I'll come out of it. I never did that year."

1963 was the low-water mark in Thomas's career as a regular player. He batted only .220, hit nine home runs, and batted in fifty-five runs. However, he managed to tie a major league record for first basemen by participating in six double plays in a nine-inning game.

I ask him why he thought it was more difficult for him to break out of a prolonged slump than it might have been for some other players.

He shrugs. "Maybe it was my temper. I'd get down on myself. I'll tell you I was pretty hard to live with in '63, with my teammates and at home and everything. It was a tough time for me. There were times when I thought I was coming out of it. You know, we all say at times, 'I can't find the holes.' When I felt like I was, I hit the ball good, but right at somebody. There was a particular week or ten days there when I did hit the ball pretty hard, but right at someone. We all have those excuses, but I never really got anything going that year. You need bloopers, and it seemed that no matter what I did nothing worked. I hate to say that I was destined for that kind of year, but yeah, it had me in a quandary. I didn't know what to do. I probably killed a hundred brain cells that year, and I didn't need to do that."

There's a slightly irritated edge to his voice, as if in recalling his worst season, the pain and deep frustration surface again. He is silent a moment while I fumble with an erratic tape recorder and try to pound it back into its record mode. Sounds of animated conversation, laughter, and ringing telephones waft into Thomas's office, and he recognizes the voice of someone outside the door. He calls to the man and tells him he wants to see him at eleven. I note that I have only twenty minutes more of the busy man's time, so abandon my tape recorder and turn on a small pocket portable, hoping it will serve me. I also prepare to jot frantic notes as a backup. Perspiring now, I beg his pardon for the problem and ask him if he thought after completing the 1962 season that he could use that year as a standard for personal performance throughout his major league career.

He nods. "Yeah. I really thought that after '62 I'm gonna hit .280 standing on my head. I'm gonna hit twenty home runs for the next seven-eight years. No, I was somewhat disappointed that I only finished with eight years in the big leagues. I saw myself playing twelve, fourteen years in the big leagues. It was very disappointing to me."

Then I ask him about 1964, the year after his disastrous season when he was traded from the Angels to Boston.

"Yeah, I was split between the Angels and the Red Sox. I think I hit .270, twenty or twenty-one home runs. Something like that." (Actually, he hit fifteen homers, accompanying sixty-six RBI.) "But even in '64 I figured I was coming back, coming out of my slump with the Angels, and then I was traded to Boston. I felt fairly good about '64. I came back and thought I had a decent year. Then '65 was really a decent year. By today's standards, it would be an outstanding year." Playing 151 games at first base and the outfield, Thomas slugged twenty-two home runs, drove in seventy-five runs, and batted .271 for the Red Sox. But the club had a disastrous season, losing a hundred games and finishing only three games out of the cellar, ahead of the then-hapless Kansas City Royals. Thomas was trade bait, as the Sox attempted to improve their standing. He was dealt to Atlanta before the 1966 season, and several weeks into the season, to the Cubs—a trade he now says signaled the end of his playing career.

Thomas takes a deep breath. "I was there for two years," he says, adding sourly, "And I guess I'd like to credit Leo Durocher for somewhat cutting my mediocre career, bringing it to a halt before it should have ended." There's a hard edge to his voice as he recalls his tenure under the fabled manager. He fairly oozes bile remembering those troubled times.

"I was coming off a pretty good year—twenty home runs, or whatever—there at Boston. I got to the Cubs and I play two or three games and Leo set me down. And hell, I was only thirty-two at the time. The Cubs were going nowhere; they didn't have that many good players and he just sat me down. We had a little go-around and I just knew from then on I was through as far as playing there. He and I did not see eye to eye. It doesn't

make any difference now, but then . . . I mean, here I am in a
ballpark where I can finally hit the ball out of it, and . . ." He
leans forward, animated, though still irritated. "I remember it, I
went one for three, one for three, and one for three. And after
that it was just spot start here, spot start there. At that time, Leo
didn't care for—did not exactly endear himself to guys who were
not regular. He loved the Santos, the Beckerts, and Adolfo
Phillips was there. He liked Kessinger. The one guy he really
didn't get along with—and you can print this—was Ernie Banks.
I think he didn't treat Ernie as nicely as he should have. And I
don't care that Ernie was at the end of the line. He did not treat
Ernie Banks very nice.

"Maybe Ernie Banks himself would not admit it, but everybody on that club knew. I'll admit Ernie was probably over the
hill at the time, but I still think the guy deserved more than what
he got from Leo Durocher. At least that's the way I look at it,
okay? I'm sure in his time Leo Durocher was a great manager. I
know there are times when the game gets away from you a little
bit, and the last few years it did get away from him. I think the
generation gap had a lot to do with it. As time goes by in this
game, you have to bend with the breeze. You don't have to break.
Players and times change, so you have to be flexible a little bit."
He pauses while I check my tiny recorder, which is making a
static-filled, whispery recording.

"Anyway," he says, resuming, "all I did was pinch-hit, play first
once in a while." He slumps back in his chair, then leans forward
again, his brow furrowing.

"We had it out one day in his office, and I knew then that I
was through as far as having a chance to play regular. You know
I'd go out there and throw batting practice to the pitchers, to the
extra men, and to the regulars. I tried to help the team. And get
this—when Leo knew I was dead tired from all this, he'd play
me. It really got to be a joke in a way. I would hate to be an extra
man and have to play my career under Leo Durocher." He makes

a long pause, rubs his chin. "If this sounds like sour grapes, so be it."

Suddenly he laughs. "I've never said this before. But I waited about six weeks before I went to see him. Santo and Billy Williams and those guys said, 'Lee, why don't you talk to him? We need your bat in the lineup.' So finally I did, and he told me he was tired of players coming in demanding to play. I told Leo that I am not demanding to play, I was just out of my own curiosity wondering what my situation was—if I am gonna get a chance. He blasted me, and needless to say, I blasted him. And when I blasted him I knew that this was the end. The whole club was listening. I had the chat with him in Houston, and he left the office door open, I think on purpose, and he blasted me and I blasted him. I couldn't have walked out of there with my head held up if I'd just walked away. In so many words I told him exactly what I thought, and it wasn't very nice." After another telephone interruption, Thomas says, "This seems like a vendetta against Leo Durocher." Then he smiles and chuckles. "But that's fine."

I notice the hour approaching eleven, and would like to ask one or two more questions before concluding, but he isn't ready to let go of Durocher.

"You know, one thing about Leo, he was an easy guy to play for when you were losing. But when you were winning, look out. He'd point out every mistake a guy was making. When you were losing it was easier. But he was the toughest guy in the world to play for when you were winning. And I'll bet that when he was back in his heyday, he *was* a hell of a manager. But . . . things just didn't bend with him."

Thomas was traded to Houston after the 1967 season, never to play on a regular basis again. His career in the majors ended when he was only thirty-two. With the Astros, in 1968, Thomas appeared in ninety games, hit one home run, had eleven RBI, and batted only .194 in 201 times at bat. The handwriting was on the wall, and Thomas had no illusions about hanging on much longer in the major leagues. But his treatment at Houston still rankles him. He was removed from the active roster on the last day of the 1968 season, denying him eight full years in the major league pension plan. I ask him if that experience makes him more sensitive to players now that he is an administrator.

He ponders the question a moment. "Well, it was somewhat a slap in the face," he says. "And I definitely think it makes me more sensitive as a general manager. I could have done that last year to a player or two here, and there was no way I would do that. I just don't think that's right. No, I would not do that to a player." He shakes his head for emphasis.

Yet baseball is first and foremost a business. Nonetheless, I am curious. So I ask, "What part does sentiment have in this game for you, having come to your present position as a former player? Being part of management, will your playing experience make it more difficult for you to make those cold decisions?" As he considers his response, I also mention that at least one future Hall-of-Famer, now in the twilight of his career, is on the Phillies roster. But modern players are reluctant to retire because of the salaries they receive. How will Thomas deal with older players who want to hang on?

"There's no doubt there is a problem when a ball club has a superstar who has come to the end of the line," he says. "Mike Schmidt's the guy you're talking about here—a shoo-in for the Hall of Fame." (Schmidt, who would go on to have a good start in 1989, slumped badly, and announced his retirement in June.)

"But you know, going from the playing ranks into this, when I get into a jam, I try to put myself in the players' place. Because, hey, look, I was a player and I would like to be handled decently. This has helped me many times, it really has. I think you have to have compassion. I think you have to be honest and fair, and tell them the way it is. I was farm director for the Cardinals for eight years, and I don't believe there's anybody that could say I've lied to them. I would rather hit home, tell 'em the truth, rather than lie in any way, shape, or form. Now hopefully, that gives me some credibility. I do hope I have that with players. I know I had it in St. Louis, and I hope I have it here."

We seem to be winding down, and I'm hoping to get in maybe one more question, but before I do, he starts in again, discussing what he thinks are major problems in baseball.

"We have a lot of problems in the area of finances. Arbitration has a lot to do with it. The salary structure is so out of whack now that you've got guys that are very mediocre players making tons of money. I think the stars should get paid, and I have nothing against anybody getting whatever they can get, but it's just so out of whack right now." He pauses, clears his throat. "But maybe more than that, I don't think there are as many young players coming out of school now going into baseball. I think the majority of them are going into football and basketball. They see a quick fix to the big leagues there, and they don't want to spend three-four years riding the buses in the minor leagues. Not as many good young arms these days, not as many athletes going into the game. And absolutely, that affects quality play on the field. I think we need to pay the younger guys more to start with to get them to come back to the game.

"Basketball and football can use the colleges as their farms. We can't. It's been proven over and over. Very rarely will a guy come out of college and step right up to the big leagues. There's a definite need for a proving ground for baseball. Baseball is the toughest of the three major sports to make it to the big leagues. You have to do so many things, and I don't care what anybody says, it's tougher to hit a round ball with a round bat, and it's tougher to throw the ball with the velocity you need to be successful. Baseball just requires more skills, I think, than football and basketball.

"College baseball is probably the equivalent of a good Class A league," he continues, enthusiastic about this topic. "Sure, there are some college players who could be Double A, Triple A players, but the overall would be an A league, and I think any one of the professional club's A teams could probably beat a good college team. I'm talking if you're playing a fifty-game schedule, the pros are gonna win. Anything can happen in two or three games, we know that. But there again, you play seven days a week in the pros, and the colleges play three days a week.

"We have to address the problem of losing athletes to football and basketball. How we do it, I guess, is to start making it more attractive—especially for the high school kids. If the truth were known, we'd probably rather go out and find a high school kid and teach him how to play the game the way we want him to play it, get them before they get too many bad habits and go from there. As it is now, most clubs are reluctant to waste a high draft choice on a high school kid because it's gonna take three-four-five years for him to arrive. So everybody's taking the college guy who's gonna be ready in a year and a half."

Lee Thomas's major league playing career ended when he was relatively young. He was unable to latch on to a big league team in 1969, but received an offer to play in Japan, where he spent that season. The following year he signed with the St. Louis Cardinals, did not make the roster, and played Triple A ball in 1970. However, the move turned out to be a good one for Thomas, because in 1971 he became a coach with St. Louis, and stayed eighteen years with the organization, including front-office stints as director of sales and promotion and traveling secretary. He was named Phillies director of personnel in July 1988, and was appointed general manager after the close of the '88 baseball season.

I have remained beyond eleven o'clock, so I turn off my tape recorder and put on my coat. We shake hands. "Well," he says, smiling, "this was fun. I kind of enjoyed reminiscing about the old days. I really enjoyed playing in the big leagues. There's nothing like it. And I feel really fortunate I had the opportunity. I feel really fortunate I've had the opportunity to get this far at the other end of baseball too."

I thank him for his time, amid jangling telephones, and a buzz of activity in the small foyer outside his office. As I gather my materials, he is already seated behind his desk, answering a phone call, and hollering off the phone for someone to come in. He needs to talk to him *now*. "By the way," he says as I walk toward the door, "feel free to call me at any time if you need anything."

I step into the foyer, and immediately four men rush by me into Lee Thomas's office. Nearly thirty years ago, the man behind the desk was a ballplayer enjoying a career season in the big leagues. He was young and his athletic future looked bright. It was, of course, but not in the way Lee Thomas may have envisioned it back in 1962. Then he was proud to have become one of the select few able to play baseball in the major leagues. Today he is in an even more select group—one of only twenty-six men who occupy the position of general manager of a major league team. And if baseball as a metaphor for life provides us with both bitter and sweet, Lee Thomas has traded the bitterness of his latter playing days for the sweetness, and the challenges, of a general managership in Philadelphia.

LEE THOMAS'S MAJOR LEAGUE CAREER

Year	Team	Games	Home Runs	RBI	BA
1961	Yankees	2	0	0	.500
	Angels	130	24	70	.284
1962	Angels	160	26	104	.290
1963	Angels	149	9	55	.220
1964	Angels	47	2	24	.273
	Red Sox	107	13	42	.257

LEE THOMAS: LOS ANGELES ANGELS, 1962

Year	Team	Games	Home Runs	RBI	BA
1965	Red Sox	151	22	75	.271
1966	Braves	39	6	15	.198
	Cubs	75	1	9	.242
1967	Cubs	77	2	23	.220
1968	Astros	90	1	11	.194
TOTALS		**1027**	**106**	**428**	**.255**

DAVE NICHOLSON:

Chicago White Sox, 1963

*". . . and then when I was traded over here I got a
chance to play. I hit the ball pretty good at times.
But it seems I really started on the strikeout binge. . . .
Those strikeouts really got to be a thing."*

If viewed from the outside, a fan's perspective, the major
league career of Dave Nicholson appears to have been fraught
with frustration. Originally signed by the Baltimore Orioles to
what was then, in 1958, considered a hefty bonus—$115,000—
Nicholson remains in the record books for the ignominious 175
strikeouts he recorded in 1963 while playing outfield for the
Chicago White Sox. Worse is the fact that he achieved his
American League record in only 126 games and just 449 times at
bat. Despite this, Nicholson also walloped twenty-two home runs
that year and drove home seventy runs—decent numbers for a
twenty-three-year-old getting his first taste of everyday play in
the major leagues. Though Baltimore's investment in Nicholson's
career didn't pan out, it seemed possible he was ready to blossom
in Chicago.

DAVE NICHOLSON: CHICAGO WHITE SOX, 1963

I never saw him play in person in the big leagues, but viewed him early on when he was with Aberdeen, South Dakota, in the defunct Class C Northern League, while I worked as public address announcer at Wade Stadium in Duluth—also a Northern League franchise. Nick's big bat and strong arm left little doubt that 1959 summer that he would star in the majors as well. He struck thirty-five home runs in '59—many of them vanishing into the horizon. He knocked in 114 runs in a league which scheduled only 120 games for its teams. He was nineteen years old then, completing his first full season as a pro player, and the crowds at the Northern League parks buzzed with anticipation every time he stepped to the plate. There was always a sense of impending drama, that something was going to happen.

In the minds of many baseball observers, though, Dave Nicholson was synonymous with failed potential. He was supposed to become a major league leader in home runs and runs batted in, and he certainly looked the part. Nicholson, at six feet two inches, carried a well-muscled 215 pounds during his playing career, which in the majors spanned parts of seven seasons. (He played his last big league game for Atlanta in 1967 when he was only twenty-eight years old.)

He was a player who had the capacity to generate enormous excitement in a ball game. His home runs were of prodigious distances, including the 1964 shot he slammed off Kansas City's Moe Drabowsky that cleared the left-field roof at Comiskey Park and landed 573 feet away, making it the second-longest home run ever hit in the major leagues. It was topped only by Babe Ruth's mammoth 600-foot wallop in 1926.

During his 1963 season—despite the strikeouts—it appeared that Nicholson was finally fulfilling the expectations Orioles manager Paul Richards had when he first saw the powerful kid from St. Louis at spring training in 1959. Certainly the offense Nick occasionally generated in 1963 provided a gleam in the eye of veteran White Sox skipper Al Lopez. There was no question that Dave Nicholson could, in players' parlance, hit the ball a ton.

Striding to the plate that year, Dave Nicholson looked like a latter-day Adonis, his massive bare arms fairly bursting through his uniform shirt. You knew if he ever got hold of a pitch, it was all over, a rocket to the moon. Nicholson launched enough rockets during his major and minor league tenures to keep baseball's top brass intrigued with his potential. The problem, though, Nicholson said, "was I didn't hit *quite* enough of them."

The irony of his major league career is that he established both personal bests and worsts during the same 1963 season. In that year, he set the league strikeout record and the major league mark. (The latter was broken in 1969 by the Giants' Bobby Bonds, who fanned 187 times and went two better in 1970 with 189 whiffs. Bonds, however, played in 157 games, batted 663 times, and hit a solid .302.) Nicholson turned in otherwise commendable numbers in 1963 and gave indication that he was perhaps beginning to get a handle on major league pitching. Despite his occasional demonstrations of power, his batting average was a slight .229. Still, his long drives and his total run production seemed sure foretokenings of solid seasons ahead.

Yet in his big league career, Nicholson appeared in just 538 games, hit sixty-one home runs, and recorded 179 RBI, while posting an anemic lifetime batting average of .212. Thus he was on the receiving end of few cheers during his checkered career and many boos—"for the strikeouts, of course." He is not bitter about any aspect of his career, though, and believes he played to his potential. He's proud of his baseball accomplishments as he reflects on his years in the game. "Gosh, I did something that millions of other people would have liked to do," he says. "I was good enough to play in the major leagues, which was always a dream of mine. If I have any regrets at all, it's that my career wasn't better. But there's nothing I can do about that. Everybody wishes they'd been better than they were."

Dave Nicholson is my age, forty-nine years old, a grandfather three times, and a sales representative for Triangle Dyes, a manufacturer of corrugated boxes. He is still heavily muscled, and carries his weight well, though he admits to weighing in at around 240. His is an athlete's physique, with a well-defined torso, the arms still sturdy, monstrous, like great logs.

His home is a pleasant rambler in Roselle, a residential suburb of Chicago. We talk in his well-appointed basement den, where there's a bar, mounted game—a deer rack, ducks—a pedestal crammed with trophies. None of the trophies, however, are for baseball. These are bowling and shooting awards, and most of them were earned by his wife, Jean. "I don't remember anybody giving trophies for baseball when I was a kid," he says, and he has kept few mementoes from his diamond career.

Seated in a comfortable leather chair, sipping a Pepsi, and lighting a cigarette, he is a congenial host, at ease with conversation. I have approached this interview needing to talk to him about his strikeout record, but at the same time wondering if he remains sensitive about it. However, his manner is so relaxed that I feel certain the issue will not be a problem. Indeed, he has already injected it into the early moments of our conversation, while I'm still trying on various nonthreatening opening gambits.

"Hell, the record's there," he says. "Anybody can look it up, and you can't run away from it. Why try?"

After he left baseball, following the 1969 season spent with Omaha in the American Association, Dave Nicholson ran his own sporting goods store for twelve years in nearby Bensonville. Next he spent three years working for another sports equipment retailer, then took his present position selling over a territory from northern to central Illinois.

Nicholson had little opportunity to demonstrate his skills during his two early stints with the Orioles. In 1960, he appeared in fifty-four games, hit one home run, drove in five runs, and batted .186. After a year with Miami in the International League,

Baltimore brought him back in 1962, and he hit nine homers, batted in fifteen runs, and averaged .173 in ninety-seven games. But the Orioles gave up on the rifle-armed kid from St. Louis and traded him to Chicago when Nicholson was only twenty-two years old—still young, even for a rookie.

"In Baltimore I was sitting on the bench, playing a defensive outfielder, because I was always considered to play pretty good outfield," he said. "I had good speed, a good arm, and when I was with them in '60 and '62 I just went in for defense most of the time and didn't get many times at bat. And then when I was traded over here I got a chance to play. I hit the ball pretty good at times. But it seems I really started on the strikeout binge and didn't play every ball game because Al Lopez knew that I'd get discouraged and down, and so he'd lay me out for a game or two, and kinda let me get it out of my mind, or whatever. Those strikeouts really got to be a thing."

Indeed. He set other infamous records, including the major league mark for most times striking out four times in one game—three in one season—and also most consecutive strikeouts—seven. The strikeout factor also drew a lot of media attention, which, Nicholson says, helped mess up his mind.

"The media doesn't let you forget it, and the fans don't let you forget it. You got it on the back of your mind all the time anyway." His demeanor does not reflect irritation that might indicate he thinks he may have been treated harshly by fans and the press. But beneath this relaxed exterior, might not Nicholson, even now, twenty-five years later, still harbor a bit of resentment at the media for heightening fans' awareness of his strikeout record? I inhale and ask him.

He smiles. "It's all in the past," he says. "What's done is done. I had a good time playing ball here. I had my best season here too, don't forget."

But when his vaunted power potential began to show some consistency in 1963—despite the mounting strikeout total—the sixties' premier slugger, Harmon Killebrew, who also piled up a considerable number of K's, came to Nicholson's defense. "Just let Nick play every day, swing the bat, and don't make an issue of the strikeouts. I'll bet he hits thirty home runs and drives in more than one hundred runs."

Those were in line with Nicholson's personal goals in the major leagues too. "I hoped I'd be able to consistently hit around twenty-five, thirty home runs a year and knock in eighty, eighty-five runs a year, and make maybe twenty-five thousand dollars a year. I'd have been satisfied with that. Today, though, twenty-five thousand dollars is nothing. The minimum is sixty-three thousand." (It was $68,000 at the start of the 1989 season.)

"Anyway, in '63, it looked like I might have a good shot at reaching those goals. At least I thought so. I would have played every day in '63. Lopez liked me. I had a good spring that year, and I more or less knew I had the regular job for the first time in my career." As a young outfielder, Nick was beginning the maturation process that ought to have brought about consistency in his game and the confidence a regular performer gains when he knows he doesn't have to be looking over his shoulder after each mistake. The job is his; the manager is going to stick with him.

Certainly Al Lopez was patient. "He left me alone more than anybody else did and gave me the opportunity to play," Nicholson says of the man he most admired and respected as a big league boss. "I thought Lopez was a super manager. Between him and the coaching staff, they tried to help you. But the main thing was I would get down on myself and just lose it for a while. But I don't blame the managers for anything that happened in my career. I blame myself." Nicholson says this without rancor, or even emotion. It is simply a statement of fact.

Yet, as he reminisces, there's little doubt he thinks coaching contributed to some of his problems as a batter. "I think I was probably overcoached," he says. "When you're eighteen, nine-

teen years old, you're not mature enough to let some of the stuff
go in one ear and out the other. You try to do this and try to do
that, and pretty soon you get confused enough to wonder how
you hit in the first place. But I don't blame that on anybody. It's
their job to coach, and of course, you want to be successful, so
you listen. But looking back on it, I was probably a better hitter
when I was twenty than when I was twenty-five."

Bonus babies like Dave Nicholson drew a lot of attention from
sportswriters during the fifties because so few of them developed
into legitimate major leaguers. But perhaps one reason was that
there was pressure on teenage kids to perform at major league
standards while they were still developing their skills. There was
also pressure on the organizations to start reaping profits on their
investments. The tendency was, then, to overinstruct these im-
mature athletes, and often the result was that the players lost
their confidence. "You forgot what you did in the first place to
get all that attention," Nicholson said. "If you had that raw talent,
sometimes a lot of coaching just caused you to lose it, or
something."

Still, in 1963 there were stretches when Nicholson says he felt
he'd found his stroke, his rhythm. "When you're in a groove the
ball looks big and it doesn't look half as fast. Your timing is there,
and a good fastball doesn't look like much. Just the opposite
when you're not hitting. A mediocre fastball looks like the guy's
throwing a hundred miles an hour. Every time he throws a
breaking ball you're fooled, or you're looking for one thing and
getting something else and nothing's going right. So what you do
is you come out and take a lot of extra batting practice. And you
try to get somebody to throw you batting practice and really put
something on the ball instead of just laying it in there. You try to
figure out what you're doing wrong, bailing out or pulling your
head away or whatever." He shifts his head as he speaks, reminis-
cent of a batter flinching at a sharply breaking curveball.

But because his slumps were less pronounced and his overall

production promising in 1963, the next spring, White Sox manager Al Lopez said it would take $750,000 to purchase Nicholson's contract, and Lopez further added that he wouldn't trade him even-up for Roger Maris, because of Nick's potential.

Upon hearing those assessments of him twenty-five years later, Nicholson smiles. "Well, that may be. I mean, everybody thought I had a lot of potential. *I* thought I had potential. I don't know how much, but I thought—I hoped I'd be a steady hitter for about ten-twelve years. You deliver good, steady numbers, and you start to make good money.

"One of my roommates was Moose Skowron. At that time I'd never played with a ballplayer who was making the kind of money he was making. He was getting forty thousand dollars a year, which to me was unheard-of. I was only making eighty-five hundred, so I didn't really have to make an adjustment when I left the game. My first year out, I made more in business than in baseball."

Nicholson grew up in St. Louis, Missouri, where his father had been a good semipro pitcher. Nicholson's first position was pitcher also. Physically, he matured early, and by the time he was fourteen, he stood six-one and weighed 190 pounds. Even then, he recalls, he was being watched by major league scouts. "They probably shouldn't have," he said, "but scouts were talking to me then. They probably thought I was a lot older than I was. Then when I was eighteen, playing in the Ban Johnson League over in Collinsville, Illinois, there were scouts from all the teams at just about every game.

"There was a twenty-one-year age limit in that league, and most of the players were from colleges. The first year I played over there there were only two high school players, myself and a pitcher. It was a good league, and we traveled, played about fifty games a season. We called it semipro, but there was no money involved.

"Anyway, I always pitched, and only played outfield a year before I started playing pro ball."

That would have been after he signed the big bonus with Baltimore in 1958. Though many teams sought his services, some did not get involved in the bidding. One team that didn't thought the Orioles had made a bad investment, and took the advice of an unnamed scout who told a wire service reporter, "I don't like Nicholson at all. I tailed him in thirteen games and he had a blind spot around his chest. I saw pitchers I wouldn't look at strike him out fourteen or fifteen times. He's a bad outfielder and always will be. He's too slow."

Nicholson sharply disputes this assessment. "The whole strike-out thing started *after* I got to the big leagues. I don't remember striking out a lot when I was younger. I was a power hitter, and power hitters will always strike out more than your contact hitters. But it was never a big thing until after I came up here."

Even so, by 1959, with Aberdeen, while he was whacking monstrous home runs, he was striking out often. It was probably overlooked in light of his record, which included tying for the league home-run title with thirty-five, and finishing second in runs batted in. His batting average also hovered around .290—excellent for a power hitter. And he also took a few turns on the mound that season.

Nicholson grins at the recollection. "Hey, I pitched great. But they didn't really want me to pitch. Earl Weaver was the manager, and he had some guys with sore arms. Earl was from St. Louis, and I had known him. I kept kidding him. 'Give me the ball, Earl, and I'll pitch.' He said, 'You haven't pitched since high school.' I said, 'Well, that was only a couple years ago.'

"So one night I come to the clubhouse and the ball's in my locker. I'm the starting pitcher. And the first time I pitched in pro ball was for Earl and I won. Struck out fourteen guys. Four-five days later, won again, struck out about eleven, and then pitched in relief a few times, and won a game in relief."

In 1966, as his major league career appeared waning, Nicholson again tried pitching. He had endured a miserable '65 with Chicago, and looked like he was going nowhere with the Houston Astros, who picked him up in a trade with the Sox after the 1965 season. So he pitched during the 1966 Instructional League winter season, forming a battery with a young catcher, Johnny Bench. "But the next year I was sold again to the Braves, and it just went by the wayside," he said. "They wanted an outfielder. But I always thought I could be a pitcher.

"One day in spring training with Baltimore, Paul Richards came up and said, 'How's your arm?' The day before we'd done a lot of throwing in the outfield, and my arm was a little sore, and I said so. He said, 'Oh, geez, if it was feeling better, we'd let you pitch a couple innings.' And I always wished I'd said, 'It feels great.' Because this was in big league spring training. I always did pretty good pitching. But if you're a pitcher who can hit, they're gonna make a hitter out of you." He mentions Babe Ruth, Stan Musial, and Dave Winfield as examples.

Nicholson may not remember many of the particulars of his career, his first base hit or his first home run, but "I remember my first at bat, and remember what I did. We were playing in Chicago. Richards pinch-hit me and I hit off Herb Score, who was one of the biggest names in baseball. I hit an infield pop-up. I've always thought, who the heck did I hit my first hit or home-run off of? I do know, though, that I was nineteen when I hit my first home run."

Prolonged slumps were endemic throughout Nicholson's career, and in three of his major league seasons he failed to hit .200. Even though he batted only .229 in 1963, that was the second-best average he recorded in the major leagues. Only the .246 he managed for Houston in 1966 was better.

But our discussion of Dave Nicholson's baseball career keeps returning to 1963, because, he says, "I thought my career had turned a corner. I was hoping that in '64 I'd come back and have a heck of a year. But I just didn't get off to a good start. Just like a lot of situations for a manager, you're trying to win. We had good ball clubs those three years I was with Chicago, and we finished second every year. So Lopez decided I was gonna play against left-handers, and somebody else was going to play against right-handers, and go with the percentages. I think the second year when I was platooned I hit thirteen, fourteen home runs and drove in somewhere in the forties." (The record shows thirteen homers and thirty-nine RBI.) Though he appeared in only ninety-seven games and had 280 times at bat, Nicholson was the third-leading home-run hitter on the Sox, with three of those blasts coming during a doubleheader on May 6, 1964. One of them, during the first game, was the famous 573-foot shot, which Nicholson says he never saw.

"I remember I had a real good day that day," he said. "It was a twi-night doubleheader and I hit it in the first game. There was always a controversy over whether or not it hit the roof. I only know I hit it a ton. The other two that day went into the upper deck. People ask me, did I see it? I didn't. As a ballplayer the ones you look at are the ones you don't think might make it and you're running, and if it doesn't go out you're gonna end up with a double or triple. But the kind you really hit, you know it's a home run when it hits the bat, so you're not paying attention."

Maybe so, but Reggie Jackson, for one, always watched his towering home runs, following the arc of the ball as it left the field. He wanted to enjoy all of it, and so do many other players. But clearly Nicholson enjoyed the attention that home run caused, and he grins as he talks about it.

"A guy and his kid were playing in a park across the street from the ballpark, and they got the ball and came in," Nicholson said. "WGN was televising the games and they had me on with Jack Brickhouse and the father and his kid between games. I gave the kid the bat I'd hit the home run with. I've still got the ball as a souvenir."

On that day, did he think he was in the groove, set to repeat or improve on his 1963 season?

"Well, yeah, but I didn't make those decisions. I still think if I had started good, had a good spring, I'd have had a good year."

If 1964, and playing part-time, proved something of a disappointment, 1965 was a year that Nicholson would probably like to forget entirely. He was out of any sort of offensive groove that season, hitting only two home runs and driving in twelve runs in just eighty-five at bats. His batting average was a career low, .153, and he fanned forty times. "Mainly I only played a little defense and didn't get many at bats. No ballplayer likes that. You don't want to sit on the bench all year. I've never been able to understand how a guy like a third-string catcher can sit on the bench all year and not play. I let the White Sox know that if they weren't going to play me they should trade me. So I went to Houston and had a super spring, hit the ball great, played pretty regular the first half-season. I was hitting about .290 and then ended up going into a platoon system. We didn't have the greatest club at Houston, and I guess I ended up the year hitting somewhere around .250. I hit a few long home runs there, and everywhere I played."

On July 5, 1966, he hit what was the longest home run ever in the Astrodome, a skyscraper blast that landed in the fourth deck. With self-deprecating humor Nicholson says, "My problem wasn't distance, it was putting my bat on the ball."

In 1967 Nicholson was back in the minors, with Richmond, a Braves affiliate in the International League. He was called up the last month of the season, appearing in ten games, batting .200 with no home runs. It was his major league swan song, though he would hang on for two more minor league seasons. The dream of succeeding in the majors didn't die easily for Nicholson. He'd had that quality season in 1963, and would hit decently after being returned to the minors.

"I kinda thought I'd get another shot at the majors after the year I had with Richmond in 1968," he said. His thirty-four home runs had led the league, and he batted in eighty-six runs. When Kansas City purchased his contract from the Braves, Nicholson thought he was on his way back. "But I had a real lousy spring and they sent me to Omaha in the American Association. I started hitting the ball real good there, though. Had a really good first half."

For the season, Nicholson hit fifteen home runs and drove in fifty runs, playing in only 75 games. "Most of that was probably in the first fifty games. I was really hot. They called me into the office and said they were looking for a good right-handed-hitting outfielder, and said if I stayed hot they'd call me up. And you know, that's the only year I ever got hurt. I had a hernia operation about midseason. Came back after five weeks off, and they were using the designated hitter in the American Association, so I tried that, but didn't get back in the swing of things after five weeks off. The hernia didn't feel like it was healing either, even during the winter. I do a lot of hunting and fishing in the off-season, and I was doing that, but it didn't seem like it was getting better. I just decided then I wanted to go into business for myself—I'd been planning it for years—so I decided that was the end. When Kansas City sent me my contract for 1970, I sent it back with a letter saying I thought it was time for me to retire.

"I would have played some more if I was single. I quit when I was thirty. During those last two years in Triple A, I had four kids, three of them in school, and they didn't like it much because I was taking them out of school and taking them to spring training, and then wherever I played, they'd have to transfer schools, and then after the season ended, we'd come back home and pull them out of school again.

"Although I wasn't old, if I'd been single I might have knocked around a couple more years in Triple A, because I liked to play." He crosses his legs, swirls the ice around in his glass. "I always liked to play."

But liking to play and being able to play baseball well are two quite different matters. Thirty years ago, Dave Nicholson was labeled by one of baseball's most astute evaluators of talent, Paul Richards, as a young player who couldn't miss. In a way, of course, Nicholson didn't miss. He made the major leagues and stayed for six full seasons. He was clearly better than a dreamer. He played, and had one decent season.

"I enjoyed it all," he says now, twenty-one years after his last appearance in a big league uniform. "I really did." There's a slight, rueful shake of his head. He speaks again, quietly, firmly. "I got into a thing where I was striking out so damn much." It was his Achilles' heel. Missing so many pitches by scant millimeters made the difference in his career. Instead of becoming one of the game's premier power hitters, he's mostly remembered by today's fans for those 175 strikeouts in 1963.

DAVE NICHOLSON'S MAJOR LEAGUE CAREER

Year	Team	Games	Home Runs	RBI	BA
1960	Orioles	54	5	11	.186
1962	Orioles	97	9	15	.173
1963	White Sox	126	22	70	.229
1964	White Sox	97	13	39	.204
1965	White Sox	54	2	12	.153
1966	Astros	100	10	31	.246
1967	Braves	10	0	1	.200
TOTALS		**538**	**61**	**179**	**.212**

BARNEY SCHULTZ:

St. Louis Cardinals, 1964

"I didn't realize the load I had on my shoulders until I walked off that mound, and we had won the pennant."

Glancing at the major league career statistics of George "Barney" Schultz in *The Sports Encyclopedia: Baseball*, one is hard pressed to find anything notable. In parts of seven seasons, the right-handed knuckleballing relief specialist won only twenty games, lost another twenty, and recorded only thirty-five saves. Yet for the final two months of the 1964 season, he was the best reliever in the game, a stopper who secured victory after victory for the surging St. Louis Cardinals as they came from seventh place on August 1 to overtake the slumping Philadelphia Phillies and win the National League pennant. While his won-loss record that year was just 1–3, Schultz posted fourteen saves—a career high—and was the finishing pitcher in many other games won by the Cards down the stretch. 1964 was the signal season in Schultz's checkered baseball career, made all the sweeter because he was an aging veteran, thirty-seven years old, who played most of that year for Jacksonville, the St. Louis farm club in the International League.

I, along with many baseball fans, rooted mightily for the old journeyman ballplayer that year, identifying with his struggle to make a career for himself as a professional athlete; identifying too with a man past his prime who was getting the job done, and was about to reap rewards for unswerving persistence, patience, and honest hard work. It was an American success story, and for those final two months of the 1964 season, Barney Schultz stole the spotlight and the headlines from some of the most notable baseball names of the times: Ken Boyer, Lou Brock, Willie Mays, Roberto Clemente, Sandy Koufax.

He did it in just thirty games, pitching forty-nine innings in August and September. But his knuckleball was virtually unhittable, and his earned run average was a sparkling 1.65.

His success was short-lived, however, and true to the pattern of his career, he spent part of the next season back in the minors again. But those final two months of the amazing 1964 season more than make up for any residual bitterness Schultz may have felt concerning his playing career, which might have been characterized as benign neglect. Schultz was a pitcher who consistently got batters out, and whose lifetime ERA was under four. Yet because he wasn't overpowering, he appeared unimpressive, even when striking out hitters. His accomplishments, therefore, seemed easy to ignore. By the time he began to appear with some regularity on major league rosters, he was already an older veteran, considered good enough to hang on until the club could find a younger arm to replace him.

A baseball man through and through, Schultz never held a job outside of the game, spending thirty-nine years in it as a player, coach, and scout. Twenty of those years were spent toiling in such minor league towns as Wilmington, Bradford (Pennsylvania), Terre Haute, Hagerstown, Macon, Des Moines, Denver, Hollywood, Columbus, Houston, Charleston, Rock Hill, Schenectady, Utica, and Jacksonville. It took him twenty-one years in organized baseball to complete three years toward the major league pension plan.

Now a youthful, vigorous sixty-three, Schultz has been retired since 1982, following a two-year stint as a pitching coach in Japan. He lives in his hometown, Beverly, New Jersey, in a comfortable two-story home, a thirty-minute drive from downtown Philadelphia and Veterans Stadium.

On a balmy, sun-splashed January afternoon, I drive to his home in a rented car. He greets me at the door, amazed that I am not wearing a coat in the dead of winter. I explain that the temperature, hovering near 50 degrees, would be considered positively springlike in Minnesota, where the day before local residents awoke to temperatures barely above zero. He invites me into his living room and indicates a straight-back wooden rocking chair for me near an outlet for my tape recorder.

He is welcoming and friendly, and before we get down to business, he introduces me to his wife, Fran, saying, "That gal really loved baseball. In fact, she misses it more than I do."

Horn-rimmed bifocals frame Schultz's large, dark oval eyes. He smiles easily and often, which accentuates the lines in his face, giving him a striking resemblance to David Frye doing his patented impression of President Lyndon Johnson.

A big man, Schultz stands six feet two and carries his weight well, perhaps a bit more than the 200 pounds he weighed in 1964. Regular rounds of golf keep him fit. He retains the effortless, graceful movements of an athlete.

I plug in my tape recorder and sit. He lights a cigarette before settling into his sofa. "Nothing formal here," he says. "Call me Barney, okay?" Then he asks me what part of Minnesota I'm from, and I tell him the Twin Cities. "I remember them well," he says, smiling at the recollection. "The old Nicollet Park there in Minneapolis, and what was it—yeah, Lexington over in St. Paul. Sure. I played there in the old American Association, you know."

Finally I begin by asking him about 1964, about why at the age of thirty-seven he would agree to play in the minors again after not making the Cardinal roster when the season started.

He exhales and shrugs. "I didn't make the roster because the team figured it wasn't going to do too much, and they wanted to give the younger players a chance," he said. "Plus Harry Walker, the manager at Jacksonville, liked me and knew what I could do. I was to go down there and pitch and be sort of a coach, with the understanding that I'd eventually become a coach with the Cardinals when I was through playing. Besides, it didn't make any difference as far as salary, so I agreed to go down there with Harry. I had a great season there too before St. Louis called me up. My ERA was under one at Jacksonville, but in my last game there before I came back up, I gave up two runs at Rochester, which brought my average over one."

He had appeared in forty-two games with Jacksonville before the Cardinals recalled him on July 31.

His presence was immediately felt, and both younger and veteran Cardinal players looked to the old man to close out victories as the team began its surge to the top. "For some reason, it was a confidence thing," Schultz said. "I remember many nights when I walked in there, looked at the hitter, and just knew I was gonna strike him out.

"Now, I have to tell you that the whole season from start to finish was significant. First, I did well at Jacksonville, and then after I got called up and started getting people out, it became such a trend in the dugout—a superstition, really—that the fellows wouldn't let me go to the bullpen until after the sixth inning. I guess there were a few games there when I didn't go to the bullpen early and we won those games. So one day I started up and they said, 'No-no—you can't go down yet. Don't change our luck.'" He chuckles. "But I can say this—I knew that I was gonna get batters out. Just about the time I got called up, the Cardinals figured that somehow they could get in the race, but they leveled off. Well, we were in New York playing the Mets and got beat two–one. From there we went to Pittsburgh, and this is really where everything developed, because it was at that point we had a good shot at the pennant."

Gene Mauch's Phillies were beginning to come apart, even though the Cardinals, still eleven games out on August 23, weren't given much of a chance by anyone—except, of course, their players.

Schultz snuffs out his cigarette. "Well, with the way the schedule remained and all, they must have felt they could pull it off. The Phillies had started losing a few and we won five in a row. It was either late August or early September. Of course, everyone remembers what happened to the Phillies. As good as we were going, we'd never have caught them if they weren't losing ball games. So this was the series that woke everyone up.

"And then the Phillies, as the month of September progressed, had their ups and downs. We were winning the majority of our games, and they were losing theirs. At one point there were about four clubs that could have won the pennant. And at that time too, I knew that I was shouldering a good bit of the responsibility to nail down wins. However, I didn't realize it until the last game of the season. We had this series with the Mets. They beat us two–one on Friday night—or did Jackson beat us one–zero on Friday night? Then they beat us the next night, but Cincinnati was doing the same thing to Philadelphia. Gosh, now I don't know—maybe we won two out of three against the Mets. I do know that first game on Friday was tough to take." St. Louis, however, with Barney on the mound at game's end, took the series finale and, with that win, the National League pennant. "I didn't realize the load I had on my shoulders until I walked off that mound, and we had won the pennant. Of course, in that game, we had a five-run lead or something. And that was it. We were there. There weren't any playoffs in those days, and I just felt like the work load was off my back. God, it was a hell of a tribute to the ball club to win it like that. It was tough for Philadelphia. For any club to lose like they lost really had to be a big disappointment."

No Phillie was more disgruntled than manager Gene Mauch. After Schultz had slammed the door on his squad in mid-September, posting his eleventh save, Mauch said, "Eleven saves in two months. That's more than Schultz has had in his whole big league career. He never saw the day he could get us out before."

Barney listens intently as I read the Mauch quote. He nods. "Well, Gene Mauch was like that. Gene Mauch—that was his way of pumping up his players, to keep them from feeling like anyone deserved success. I don't think there was anything personal there. There are remarks that are made when a guy's losing, and certainly many people have come back and said nasty things about Gene Mauch. I mean, all the opportunities he's had to win, and he's never won a pennant. That's all part of the game. Right after he made that remark, it was hell for them because they couldn't touch me." The old reliever smiles and lights another cigarette.

I ask if he did anything differently in '64 than he had in his previous, relatively uneventful stops in the majors with Detroit and the Cubs. "Well, I did have a tighter grip on the ball. I popped my wrists more, as in a fastball. That seemed to cut down on my strikeouts, but I got 'em out." He grins broadly, then his smile dissolves and he assumes a businesslike countenance.

"This business about saves," he says, exhaling, "was something you didn't dwell on like you do today. And I think the rules constituting a save are different today than they were back then. Relievers pitched two-three innings then, not just to one batter or two. That's why when you look at the stats of a relief pitcher, you can't judge it by the won-loss record, because it doesn't mean the same thing as it does for a starter. And also, you have to consider the innings he pitched too. What kinds of situations were there when he came into a ball game. There's almost always a lot of pressure. In '64, as it happened, they needed me and went with me."

Barney Schultz was in organized baseball from 1944 through 1982. He was originally signed by Jocko Collins and the Philadelphia Phillies to a contract with Wilmington, Delaware, in the Class B Interstate League. "I was signed right out of Burlington County High School," he said. "And I'm sure we got some sort of record. There were three of us on that team, Eddie Miksis, Sam Calderone, and myself, who made it to the big leagues. Now there's probably cases where one high school sent maybe more guys to the big leagues, but have you ever heard of three guys from one high school team making it?"

Schultz spent two seasons in Wilmington and in the second year hurt his throwing arm. "I got over the sore arm," he recalled. "I could pitch, but I lost some speed, so I had to change my style and perfect the knuckler. It wasn't that I didn't know how to throw the knuckleball before that. I just didn't have to use it. I could always grip the knuckleball, even when I was first signed by the Phillies. When I was a kid, I always had a ball and glove in my hand. There was an older fellow who lived next door, and he could throw it. He could make it dance. And that, I guess, was the biggest help I ever had, because nobody else ever worked with me on the knuckleball. I'd throw one once in a while in high school, but used it like a change. I didn't fool around with it much, though I always had the good feel of it. But developing it as a successful pitch is another thing." He pantomimes, showing me his grip and his release.

"That second year in Wilmington, when I hurt my arm, I was having a good year. And I was pitching a ball game at Lancaster, and it was a real hot night. I threw a pitch and I got pain in my shoulder. I finished the game and we went back to Wilmington that night and the next day I couldn't tie my shoelaces. In those days they didn't have the means they do today to take care of you, so I just went back to pitching, but it kind of messed up my whole season. I think I finished something like eleven–fourteen that year, and when I got hurt I was like nine–five or nine–six, which was good at the time.

"They called me into the office just before the last game of the season, talked to me. Told me they knew I had difficulty with my arm. But they didn't want me to go to any doctors. Just wanted me to go home and get a good rest in the off-season. Today a guy in the minor leagues hurts his arm, he's up with the big team having their doctors work on him. Experts checking him out. You had a so-called trainer then. And that was it. So I did that, and went to spring training the next year, and first started throwing. But I couldn't throw a ball to home plate. That was 1946. I was with Utica in spring training. So I had to struggle for a couple years with that arm and the pain kinda left and I'm working on the knuckleball—actually, all my stuff—you know? It was perseverance, I guess you might call it. But I was doing what I wanted to do, making a living, and that was enough. I mean, in those days, God almighty, it was amazing. I remember in those days we'd go out on the road and get three dollars a day meal money. Can you imagine eating on three dollars a day today? But you know what you could do in those days? You could have a full-course meal—breaded veal cutlets and all the works for about a dollar fifteen. So you really ate good. But you know what we paid for a room?" He is animated now, speaking loudly, with much enthusiasm. "They always had homes—and I'll never forget going to Wilmington when I was a young boy—and this woman charged me five dollars a week. Beautiful little home she had, and she said, 'You can use any room up there you want. Use the refrigerator too.' Gosh, there's things now that no one's ever read about from that era. You know what I mean? It was oh so much different then." He pauses. "You know, I oughta write a book about all that. That's a whole different era. The minor leagues were so different then, and so were the big leagues, of course. Really, I think it would make an interesting book, don't you?" He pauses, watches the smoke rise from his cigarette in the ashtray, his mind wandering back through time to perhaps the forties, a time of innocence and promise in America, a time of what seemed to be unlimited potential and a future of endless sunshine and good times. Finally he looks up at me.

"Fran and I get married, and I get to the majors in 1955. But I have to go down to the minors, and I'm making the kind of money I can't make in any other place. People in 1955 weren't making nothing. I had no alternative but to stay with it. I guess basically the main reason was that it was gonna be my career. I'd stay with it no matter what."

He shakes his head. "I'm not a millionaire, but I'm doing okay." He chuckles.

"You know, speaking of money," he starts in again, "back years ago I can remember when the major league minimum was fifty-five hundred dollars. At that time there weren't too many workingmen making fifty-five hundred dollars a year. I think that was an altogether different structure. When I broke in forty-five years ago—that was before the war was over—there were quite a number of minor leagues. And then when the war did end you had quite a number of players coming back out of the military, so all the minor leagues started operating again. That was the golden era of minor league baseball.

"And the reason minor league baseball was so successful was we didn't have television. I can remember pitching in Denver in 1951 and 1952. Those years at the end of the forties and into the fifties, Denver used to outdraw a couple major league clubs. I was a starter then in '52 and had one of my best years, and ended up in Denver before I was traded to the Cardinal organization. You could see how television affected attendance in the minor league parks. Some of those little old cities, they used to have outstanding times at the ballpark. But pretty soon they'd stay home and watch baseball on television." He shakes his head. Television represented progress that an old minor league pitcher seems to resent somewhat. He's fond of reminiscing about baseball in the bushes, the bus rides, the stale-sweat smell of dank locker rooms, the pungent odor of cigar smoke wafting over the fields, and yes, the roar of the crowds that are now absent from minor league parks.

I try to bring him back to 1964, and I ask him to tell me about getting into a groove where his confidence was such that he knew he could handle a batter or particular situation, knew he would be successful.

He nods. "I think you're talking about something that many, many players have thought about over time. I felt that way myself, and I felt it with many, many hitters—against some of the better hitters in the game. For example, Orlando Cepeda, one of the better hitters of our time. Orlando couldn't hit me, he couldn't touch me. He once told me he came to bat sixteen times against me and I struck him out fifteen times. Well, he was traded over to the Cardinals later when I was the Cardinals' minor league pitching coach. I happened to come into St. Louis on occasion, and I was in the clubhouse saying hello to everyone. This one particular evening I walked in there after batting practice and Orlando spied me coming through the door and he came over and grabbed me by the hand, and he wanted everybody to hear. And he made me get up on one of the trunks there in the clubhouse, and he said, 'This is the greatest pitcher of all time. I cannot hit this man. I never could hit this man.'" He laughs loudly. "But this is just one of those things. I think most pitchers who've enjoyed success at one time or another have this feeling that they can't lose.

"I can reflect back to the last year I pitched. I was at Tulsa. I was coaching at that time too, in 1966. Charley Metro was the manager at Tulsa, the Cardinals Triple A club. Well, we were grooming young players, and when one would come up from one of the lower minors, I would go off the active list. I'd just coach. That went on off and on all season. Finally, we were going down the stretch, and Charley said, 'Barney, you're coming on now, and you're staying on. We gotta win this division and get into the playoffs.' Which we did, and played Seattle. But anyhow, to make a long story short, we're out in Seattle and Charley brings me into the game. Men were on second and third. The winning run was at the plate. A left-handed hitter and one out. You don't ordinarily walk the winning run, but some managers will gamble and some will walk him intentionally. So Charley said, 'What do you think, Barn? You want to pitch to him or walk him?' I said, 'Well, you're the manager—you call it.' Dave Ricketts was the catcher, and he said, 'Okay, put this guy on and strike out the next two.' And that's exactly what I did, struck out two on seven pitches. Charley never got over that. We laughed and talked and made a big issue over it. It's something that happens. Why it doesn't happen more often is anybody's guess."

I ask him if he ever felt the reverse of ultimate confidence, and sensed that the batter "owned" him, and that he couldn't possibly get that batter out.

He nods as he lights another cigarette. "Well, I've had the feeling through the years that it wasn't a case of the guy crushing the ball, but it was a case, well, this guy, if he gets a base hit the ball game's over. Or, if this guy gets a base hit I'm out of here. So what a pitcher actually does, and what everyone does, is we put more of a load on our shoulders. Load yourself and you get uncomfortable. And why you get into that kettle of things, God only knows."

As the 1964 pennant race tightened late in the season, Cardinal manager Johnny Keane, supremely confident, said, "We're going to win the pennant now. Our starting pitching is in great shape. . . . And of course, there's always Barney. That old guy's got a rubber arm. If you pitch him in short stints, he can work almost every day."

He didn't work every day, but he was ready and delivered when it counted. He pitched in eight of the Cardinals' last twelve games that season, and was the man Keane and the players counted on when a crucial ball game was on the line.

Durability was always one of Schultz's strengths. During 1962, when he was with the Cubs, he pitched in nine consecutive games, tying the major league mark at the time. "I would have made it ten, easy, because that tenth game went into extra innings," he said. "But what happened was I pulled a muscle in my leg." He rubs his leg and grimaces, recalling the strain, and how it cost him entry into the record books.

"At that time the Cubs were run by coaches, rather than a manager. They shared responsibilities. I didn't think it was a bad system. Anyway, we were in New York, playing in the old Polo Grounds, and it was getting close to midnight. I entered the game, and Elia Chacon dropped a bunt to the left of the mound, which I went over and fielded easily and threw him out, but I pulled a calf muscle. I wasn't taken out of the game or anything. In those days we pitched with pain. But it put me on the shelf. Next day I could hardly maneuver." He chuckles without mirth and shakes his head. "Sure enough, we had a long ball game the next day—twelve or thirteen innings—and I would have pitched and set the record, which I had tied with Elroy Face."

He laughs now. "Charley Metro used to walk around and talk to the fellows in batting practice and when the pitchers would be running or out shagging in the field. He was one of the coaches under that system. He came out to left field one day when I was shagging on a hot day. 'Barn,' he says, 'how ya feeling? How's things goin'?' I said, 'Gee, I'm not gettin' much work, Charley.' He said, 'Just hang in there.' So as things developed, about my fifth straight game now, Charley comes to me and he asked me, 'Barney, are you getting enough work *now*?'" Schultz enjoys a hearty laugh.

He stands up. "Say, you want a cup of tea or coffee?"

I opt for tea and follow him into the kitchen, where he places cups of water and tea bags into the microwave oven. While we wait I ask him about his play in the 1964 World Series. Though St. Louis beat the Yankees in seven games, Schultz's performance was a far cry from his pitching during the pennant drive. He gave up nine hits and eight runs in just four innings of work, and was the losing pitcher in game three, giving up the game-winning home run to Mickey Mantle.

He talks as we return with our cups to the living room. "About all I can say is that the Series was anticlimactic for me. I guess I just ran out of luck. I can't pinpoint any reason for my showing. The pressure was in winning the pennant, and I felt that enormous pressure on me to save those ball games in the late innings. Now you earlier talked about feeling negative about things or positive in knowing you could do things. Well, we won the first game of the Series. Sadecki started and went six innings, and I finished the next three innings. At that point, even in that game, I didn't feel anything like I had before. There had been so much pressure, I guess it took its toll. Others I've talked to outside of baseball—a doctor in St. Louis told me one time when we were discussing things like that, he said, 'I've been a doctor a good many years, and the same thing happens in the medical profession. You go along in an operation, and you get over the hump and' "—Barney exhales deeply—" 'you're saved.' That's how I felt, because the Series wasn't really my best pitching. We were there, we got there. After the first game . . ." He shrugs, lets the thought drift. "But it was a great Series. Good pitching. Bad pitching. There was good hitting, bad hitting. Everything was in that Series. A lot of home runs. It was a seven-game Series. The Yankees had a heck of a ball club, as you might remember from back then. It was a good victory. Our ball club, comin' from where they did—and here I was pitching in Jacksonville most of the season—and now here we are at the top. Just about every fellow who's ever played would like to have been there. No matter how successful they've been they'd like to be in the World Series. It was just a great feeling." He sighs and smiles.

He is not wearing his World Series ring, though, and I ask about it.

"I got two," he said. "One for the year I was coaching and we played Boston. I just never put it on today, I guess. I wear it all the time. That '64 ring, it's just like it was the day I got it almost. Everything neatly detailed on it. Just yesterday I showed it to about twenty people at the church."

But life at the top, though sweet, was all too brief for Barney Schultz. While he pitched in thirty-four games for the 1965 Cardinals, he couldn't duplicate his '64 success. He won two and lost two, saving only two for the Cardinals, who tumbled to seventh place under new manager Red Schoendienst. And Schultz was returned to the minors late in the season. "Yeah, I had to go back down near the end there because they wanted to bring up two catchers. Mike Shannon got hurt, and they had to bring up a catcher, so they sent me to Jacksonville. Then I came back up. Didn't mean much, because the club wasn't going anywhere. Naturally, I didn't want to go back down. But as I reflect back, I was one of the older guys, and they're gonna look at these young pitchers. A guy can't go on forever. But that was Red's first year. He had a big load to carry, and he took over a ball club that had won the pennant the year before, and it totally collapsed. Sore arms, injuries, what-have-you. You had to play some of your players differently than you wanted to, and all that contributes too. So the club wasn't too successful that year."

It was Barney's last hurrah in the major leagues. The next season he was back at home in the minors, pitching and coaching at Tulsa, still able to get kids out with that baffling knuckler. But at age forty, not anticipating a return to the big leagues, he decided to retire as an active player.

Still, Barney Schultz remained on somebody's baseball roster until the end of the 1977 season as a coach. He followed that with three years as special assignment coach with the Cubs, before putting in two years as pitching coach of the Osaka Hawks in Japan under manager Don Blasingame.

As we talk about baseball in Japan, he rises. "Come here, I'll show you something," he says. He leads me to his den. There is an impressive white Japanese tapestry with red and gold trim in the corner near the fireplace. "Fran picked that up over there," he says. Also displayed is a photo plaque of the 1964 World Champions, and another commemorating his selection to the South Jersey Baseball Hall of Fame, in which he'd recently been inducted along with former major leaguers Ray Narleski, Eddie Miksis, and Rawley Eastwick.

We look over old photographs, and again he speaks fondly of his wife's tolerance of his chosen career. "Baseball is tough on a household," he says. "But my whole family was baseball-oriented, so it was never any problem."

We returned to the living room, our interview nearly over. He asks if I'd like more tea. I decline. I ask what he's done since leaving the Osaka Hawks.

He grins. "I came back home December eighteenth, 1982, and I said to Fran, 'Well, I'm gonna take this year off.' And she said, 'All right, do what you want to. You're the boss.' Well, I liked '83 so much I stayed with it." He laughs. "But you know, I think Fran misses the game something awful. She'd like me to get back in, I think." But he's content these days playing golf, visiting friends, taking life easy.

Like many long-retired baseball players, Barney Schultz is not forgotten by fans, who still write him requesting autographs. Also like a growing number of his fraternity, he's not always anxious to comply. "I've had to slow down on the autographs. It's now a big business. I used to sign them all. But recently I've had guys send me ten to twelve cards, they'd send me a dozen bubble-gum cards. What I do now, if I get a stack of them, is I'm beginning to look at the other side. They're really using you. I'm signing them and they're trading them off and having their conventions and all. I don't mind doing this once in a while for a group of people." He shakes his head. "It really got obnoxious after a while. I'd be gone a couple weeks, and I'd come back and have a stack of mail—" He holds his hands about ten inches apart. "Here, I'll show you something. Here's two I haven't answered." He hands me an opened envelope. "That's very simple there. A simple request for an autograph. With people like this, sometimes if I have an extra postcard picture, I'll send that along too. That's all he wants, that little card there. Now," he says, handling me another letter, "here's a guy and he's got a form letter here and he's sending that to everybody, requesting signatures on more than a dozen cards and photos. If I respond and tell him okay, he'll send me about fifteen or twenty. Now if you take all those requests, take all my time for people who are gonna be selling and trading these cards, why some days, that'd be all I ever did. Still, for years and years I used to sign them all."

I snap off the tape recorder and close my notebook and thank Schultz for his time. We shake hands. "I'd have to say I owe everything to baseball," he says, holding the door for me.

I back out of the driveway, and wave one last time to the hero of the 1964 pennant race, who stands in the window, returning my wave, his arm around his wife.

BARNEY SCHULTZ'S MAJOR LEAGUE CAREER

Year	Team	Games	Won	Lost	Saves	ERA
1955	Cardinals	19	1	2	4	7.80
1959	Tigers	13	1	2	0	4.50
1961	Cubs	41	7	6	7	2.69
1962	Cubs	51	5	5	5	3.81

Year	Team	Games	Won	Lost	Saves	ERA
1963	Cubs	15	1	0	2	3.67
	Cardinals	24	2	0	1	3.60
1964	Cardinals	30	1	3	14	1.65
1965	Cardinals	34	2	2	2	3.86
TOTALS		**227**	**20**	**20**	**35**	**3.63**

BILL GRABARKEWITZ:

Los Angeles Dodgers, 1970

"Steve [Garvey] wasn't getting many hits, and we weren't winning games. . . . So they put me in at third base and I went two for four and hit a home run. So they said, 'Well, let's leave him in there and play him tomorrow.' I got another two hits. I kept getting one, two, three hits every game, and they kept me in there. After two weeks they sent Steve Garvey down to the minors."

Bill Grabarkewitz likes to ask a baseball trivia question: "Who got the hit after Pete Rose in the 1970 All-Star game? Everybody remembers it was Jim Hickman who got the third hit with two outs in the twelfth." That game-winning single by Hickman won the game for the National League, but the play is remembered more for the lick Pete Rose put on American League catcher Ray Fosse while crossing the plate with the winning run. That collision spelled the end of Fosse's career as a front-line player in the major leagues.

"I'm standing on second base when they show that collision at home on sports highlights clips," Grabarkewitz says. "I singled off a Clyde Wright fastball, and gave Hickman the chance to win the game."

That game and indeed all of the 1970 season provided career

highlights for a twenty-three-year-old kid from Lockhart, Texas, who was playing his second season in the big leagues. He would be out of the majors five years later, only twenty-eight years old, a victim of overzealous coaching that ruined his batting stroke, and of severe leg injuries that plagued him throughout his career. At age forty-two, he lives in Dallas, a success in business, earning a salary far greater than the $42,500 which was his top pay in the big leagues. These days Grabarkewitz is a regional director for an insurance firm, overseeing 550 agents.

It is seven forty-five on a cold, gray December morning when we meet at the airport Holiday Inn for breakfast. He has the appearance of a business executive, sartorially subdued in a gray charcoal suit, white shirt, and maroon tie and matching suspenders. His brown hair has a few gray flecks. He smiles easily and often, and is a comfortable interviewee, perhaps because of his own experience as a journalist. Back in the late 1960s he was an off-season sportswriter for the *San Antonio Light*.

He is trim, but does not appear athletic. He never was a big man, five feet ten, weighing about 175 pounds. He's interested in this book, and in writing in general, and tells me about a friend who's writing a baseball story screenplay.

Football frequently encroaches in our conversation, as Herschel Walker had recently been traded by the Cowboys to the Vikings, and Grabarkewitz is an avid fan. He mentions that his son Neal is a lineman on an undefeated high school team that has reached the Texas state championship quarterfinals. Football seems a natural conversational gambit anyway, since this hotel is mini-camp headquarters for Tex Schramm's new International League of American Football. The public spaces are redolent of analgesic balm, and heavily muscled athletes are stretching and taping in the lobby, which has been converted into a gigantic locker room.

As our waiter pours the first of nearly a dozen cups of coffee, I ask Grabarkewitz to tell me about his baseball beginnings.

He leans forward, glances at my recorder, and asks if it's

working before launching into a reminiscence. "Well, I started out in Little League. In fact, when I was ten years old, I put a lot of pressure on myself, because when people asked what I wanted to be when I grew up, I always said I wanted to play baseball for the Los Angeles Dodgers. I continued on through Babe Ruth League and high school. I hit something like .400 my senior year and got something like three or four scholarship offers. But they were all withdrawn when the schools heard about my size." He chuckles. "Back in high school I started out at five-five-and-a-half, and weighed a hundred and forty pounds soaking wet.

"But I ended up at St. Mary's University in San Antonio, and made All-American my second year. We played all the Southwestern Conference schools—good competition. So I signed with the Dodgers after my sophomore year." He laughs again. "I had to do a little trickery to do it," he says, grinning. "Atlanta was very interested in me. By now I had grown to almost five-ten, and put on twenty-five pounds. Atlanta said they were going to draft me. But I only wanted to play for the Dodgers. I'd committed to them early in my life, so I told the Atlanta scouts, 'If you draft me, you'll be wasting a choice, because I'm gonna stay in college. I'm not playing pro ball, period.' Anyway, in about the ninth or tenth round I got picked by the Dodgers. I remember the first eight round picks didn't ever make it to the Dodgers. Bill Russell, Ted Sizemore, and I were three in a row in later rounds who did make it. We were nine-ten-eleven, or ten-eleven-twelve, I don't remember."

He pokes a forkful of scrambled eggs into his mouth as I signal our waiter for more coffee.

He chews solemnly, takes a bite out of a muffin. "I was fortunate, because I believe that when a lot of players get to the minor leagues, they have equal ability. But you have to have the opportunity, and you have to have a good organization and good coaches. I had those." He reported to the Tri Cities franchise in the rookie Northwest League for his first exposure to pro baseball.

"Duke Snider was the manager and Roger Craig the pitching coach. We had a real good team, played an 82-game schedule, and won the pennant by sixteen games. Snider was a good manager, but a lot of good coaches were not good ballplayers, and vice versa. The great coaches understood the problems. Roger Craig was a great hitting instructor for me, because he didn't know anything about hitting. He said, 'Go up there, be aggressive as hell. You can't walk to the big leagues. Go up there swinging, score a lot of runs, and make my pitchers look good.' "

Grabarkewitz did. He hit with authority throughout his minor league tenure, which included stops in Albuquerque (where he suffered a serious broken ankle) and Spokane before his arrival with Los Angeles in 1969. "I had a great minor league career in two and a half years, made the all-star teams. Then the Dodgers called me up from Spokane. I arrived at Dodger Stadium, and of course I was as nervous as hell. But I remember I went oh for three that night. Lined out to third, struck out, and grounded out. The next day the Dodgers' batting instructor, Dixie Walker, had me out taking extra batting practice and changing my hitting style completely. He wanted me to be like Felix Millan. He gives me a real heavy bat, and has me choke up, open up my stance. And I still wonder today why they ever hire instructors like that. You'd think they'd say, 'Hey, if you got here like this, why change things?' Walker would have made Willie Mays a Punch and Judy hitter. Because Walker was a Punch and Judy, he believed everybody should be a Punch and Judy. I always resented that. Matter of fact, he tried to do that to a lot of guys—good hitters. Garvey, I think, started out tremendously slow. Because when he came up, Dixie Walker was the hitting instructor. His philosophy was 'Don't hit any home runs. It'll ruin you. Hit a home run and you're screwed up for life, because you'll want to hit more.' Now Dixie, bless his heart, was a real nice old man, but in 1969 I hit only .092. I went six for sixty-five." He shakes his head at the recollection, but I'm impressed that he recalls the negative stat so precisely. I later check the records and discover he is correct.

"I could probably go down in baseball history as the worst pinch hitter who ever played the game. That's what I predominantly did in '69. Sat on the bench and pinch-hit. I think young guys have a much harder time playing once in a while than some of the veterans. A veteran player is a much better pinch hitter. Also, in '69, Tommy Lasorda lied to the Dodgers when I got recalled. I was hitting .429 or something like that at Spokane. Al Campanis asked him how I was doing. Tommy says, 'Great.' Al asks about my leg, because I'd broken it the year before. 'Oh, he's running great.' Which was a lie. I mean, my leg was swelled up like this." He holds his hands apart, indicating the size of a small watermelon. He shakes his head and chuckles.

"I had to get taped up twice a game. Anyway, Tommy says, 'When you go down there, don't you dare limp.'" Another chuckle. "Geez, I couldn't run. And that was really my biggest asset—my speed. '69 was a waste. All I felt that year was pain and travel."

I cough around an overly dry muffin, gulp coffee, and ask him how, given those stats, he managed to make the roster the following year.

He nods, picks at his bacon, signals for more coffee, clears his throat. "They knew from my years in the minors what I could do. I'd hit quite a few home runs too. I won the glove at my position in the minors. So they maybe figured 1969 was one of those things. Plus, in 1970, I really wanted to make the team. That was the priority."

Coffee arrives. Cups are refilled. I need to use the rest room. Grabarkewitz, bladder of steel, raises his cup.

Upon my return, he asks if we were talking about 1970, and I ask him to start at the beginning of the year.

"The Dodgers had gotten Maury Wills back in a trade, so my chances of playing shortstop were nil at that time. Yet I never considered myself a third baseman. The year before, Ted Sizemore was Rookie of the Year at second base. So that really didn't leave a lot of positions left. I went to spring training, and they stuck me at third base, backing up Steve Garvey. He'd had a real good year in the minors, and he was going to get every opportunity. But I had to prove myself.

"I knew I wasn't going to be able to play shortstop. I couldn't take the stress on my leg in that position yet. I had a really good spring training, though. Ankle had started to bounce back. I felt I could run almost as fast as before. At the end of spring training, I was the fastest guy on the team. I could beat Willie Davis at sixty yards. In fact, later that year after I beat out two hits in St. Louis, Richie Allen grabbed me when I came back to the bag and said, 'Man, I'm gonna have to check you out. You run too fast for a white boy.' Then when I proceeded to take my lead, he grabbed my belt and held me. I called time and told the umpire. He said, 'You can't do that. What's the matter with you?' Richie said with a straight face, 'Well, the man [his manager] told me to hold him on.'" We both laugh. "Richie was a funny guy." He lingers in reminiscence, a smile insinuating itself across his lips.

"Anyway, I hit about .350 in spring training, and hit three or four home runs. The season started and I was on the bench, and I understood why. But Steve had problems, and I think a lot of Bobby Valentine's early problems could be blamed on Dixie Walker trying to change things. I think it was a tremendous mistake to have him as hitting instructor, as nice a man as he was. He tried to change everybody.

"About the first five or six games, Steve hit the ball pretty good, but I don't think he got many hits. Steve wasn't getting many hits, and we weren't winning games. If you don't hit, and the team's winning, that's not so bad, but when you're losing and not getting hits, that really magnifies the situation. So they put me in at third base and I went two for four and hit a home run. So they said, 'Well, let's leave him in there and play him tomorrow.' I got another two hits. I kept getting one, two, three hits every game, and they kept me in there.

"After two weeks they sent Steve Garvey down to the minors." Grabarkewitz laughs. "It was funny, because here I am, not really a third baseman, and I'm playing third base in the big leagues. At that time in Dodger Stadium, they put crushed brick on the infield. They've taken it out now, though. But the best third basemen who ever played in the major leagues, Clete Boyer, Doug Rader, guys like that, will tell you the worst place to ever play third base was at Dodger Stadium. Far and away. In fact, most of them played up on the grass, even with the bag. Because they felt that once that ball was on that brick, they couldn't get it. They had veteran years, so they could play wherever they wanted. No one was going to tell them where to play. With me, the coach would say, 'Hey, back up.' I was a rookie, so they kept backing me up. It was also rough around shortstop, but for some reason it wasn't so bad at second base. But it was possible to lose ground balls in the lights at that old stadium. Once Ron Santo was hit on the head on a high hopper." Bill stands by the booth, indicates a hopper bouncing off the turf and ascending into the stratosphere out of the arc of the stadium lights. "Pieces of ground would move out there. There'd be pits and chunks like a mine field.

"So I played third." He empties another cup of coffee, which is immediately refilled by the waiter. He stares straight ahead for a few seconds, gathering his thoughts. Finally he speaks again. "Confidence is about ninety percent of baseball. There's not a great amount of difference in ability at the big league level. Staying healthy, having the opportunity to play, and having confidence are the important things. A lot of players may show confidence outwardly, but they really don't have it. If you have it, you feel invincible; you can go out and get a hit. Most of 1970, wherever I went I felt I could hit anybody."

He begins a digression into what happens when a hitter is

going well, as opposed to when he slumps. "Thing is, when you're hitting well, you're hitting with both eyes. Whenever you're hitting you've got to see with both eyes. If you move your head even a little bit"—he is in his stance, lifting his head slightly—"you don't see the last three feet of the ball when you're hitting with one eye. If you've seen pictures of a hitter, you'll notice that both eyes are on the ball when it contacts the bat. But hitting instructors should always just say, 'Keep your eyes on the ball, take an easy stride, be aggressive, and run like hell.' But nobody's going to pay an instructor to just say that. They think they have to do something to earn their salaries, and they wind up messing up a lot of hitters.

"When you get to the major leagues, you basically don't need a hitting instructor. If you're hitting with one eye, you ought to know—hey, I'm pulling my head. A lot of hitting instructors are really adult baby-sitters who are there to pat people on the head and say, 'Hang in there. Everything's gonna be all right.'"

He grows silent again, but is smiling slightly. "You ever hear of the Little League prayer?" Before I respond, he chuckles and says, "'Oh, God, please don't let him hit it to me.' I was like that at the All-Star game. I was so nervous I think I changed sweatshirts twice before I ever got in the game. Ron Santo was the starter that year, even though he was hitting only around .210 or something like that. But I was selected as a third baseman, which was a joke. Because in the month and a half prior to the game, I had played nothing but short and second. I got to the All-Star game and didn't take infield practice. I never even got to make any throws to first base from third. There's a big difference between third and short. It was kind of funny, because Willie McCovey went in at first base and he said, 'Just keep it out of the second deck and I'll catch it.'

"I was nervous as hell, but during the first seven innings there hadn't been any balls hit over there, so when I got in the game I thought I was safe. Claude Osteen was out there pitching, and sure enough, four of the first five balls were hit to me. McCovey caught them all. That was a great game and I really enjoyed it. But to show you how nervous I was, on that base hit I got to left field, the writers asked me later what pitch I'd hit. I said a slider down and in. Saw a replay later and it was actually a fastball outside."

He laughs again, sips coffee. "I was in another world out there. I was like a kid going to his first baseball game. I was just happy to be on the field with those guys."

During the first three months of the season, there wasn't a hotter hitter in the league than Billy Grabarkewitz once he began playing regularly. At the All-Star break he was batting .376, and it seemed even if he endured a major slump he would still end the season around .300.

However, after the July classic, he had a horrendous August. He blames this on more interference from Al Campanis and Dixie Walker.

The old infielder tugs at his tie, then cradles his coffee cup between his hands and regards a cold sleet slanting against the window. He shakes his head. "What was amazing was the day after the All-Star game, which was a day off, Campanis calls me into his office and says, 'You're doing real good, but you know you need to cut down on your strikeouts.'

"So he got Dixie Walker to go out and work with me. I'm hitting .376 and Dixie wants to change my whole hitting style again. And he says, 'First of all, you need to quit swinging for home runs.' He switched me to a heavier bat again, and it's like I didn't have a choice. I'm being told to do this. So in the month of August, I don't think I struck out six times. And I think I hit .101. At the end of the month, I said something to Dixie, which I feel bad about now, because he's deceased. I told him that his whole thing was screwing up the way that I swing, and the way that I play, and I wanted to back to the lighter bat and be aggressive again. And if I strike out, I strike out. If I screw up, I want to do it my way. I went back to that bat, and the last month I did real good again—hit home runs, struck out a lot, but got base hits. I still had one of the best on-base percentages in the league. I don't remember what it was, but I think I had a hundred and some walks too."

1970 was a solid offensive season for Grabarkewitz, whose final batting average was .289, while his seventeen home runs led the Dodgers. He also knocked in eighty-four runs, third on the Dodgers behind Wes Parker and Willie Davis.

More coffee is poured. Grabarkewitz is chuckling softly, looking down at the table. Finally his gaze lifts. "I'll never forget the first time I went up against Gaylord Perry, who is a hell of a nice guy. I really liked him. But facing him was about as strong a battle as you could get. First time I faced him I went two for four, and my second hit knocked him out of the game. I was on first base and as he was walking to the dugout he cussed me. 'You little shit, you're not gonna get another hit off me.' And you know something, I must have gone another fifteen, eighteen at bats before I did get another hit. And then I got a home run.

"Funny thing, though, later Dick Dietz got traded to us. And he said, 'You always had trouble with Gaylord, didn't you?' 'Yeah, he's tough,' I said. 'He kept throwing that little slider and all I could do was beat that damn thing into the ground.' Dick said that he didn't throw me anything but spitters after that first game. No wonder I couldn't hit that crap. Marichal was tough on me, and I hit a couple homers off him. And Dietz—I don't think he liked Marichal much, because one time after he had thrown behind my head, I got a single off him. Next time Dietz said, 'Be ready first pitch.' As soon as he threw it it went right over my head."

I ask if any other pitchers were particularly troublesome for him in 1970.

"Yeah, we only had to face Bob Gibson one time because of the way the schedule worked out. Even at the end of his career he still threw good. In St. Louis, he strikes me out on three pitches. Next time out, I think he strikes me out on three pitches again. Now about the seventh or eighth inning, I think we're behind two–one, and all of a sudden we get two hits in a row. Now I haven't touched Gibson yet, and their manager, Red Schoendienst, had a couple guys warming up. There were two outs, and I notice him signaling the bullpen to hurry up, get them ready. Gibson doesn't like it when a batter stalls, and usually you don't do it when a pitcher is tiring, but I haven't touched him yet, so I'm stepping out, calling time, going after more pine tar. Because I know they want to get their relief pitcher in there. I'm stalling all I can to give them a chance to bring in somebody else. Finally, out comes Schoendienst and he brings in George Culver, and I'm almost wanting to go over there to kiss him. I hit a double, knocked in both runs, and we win the game. Guess who gets the loss? I beat Gibson and I never touched a ball he threw." Grabarkewitz laughs heartily.

He obviously relished winning the mind game with Schoendienst that day, but other memories are also vivid too. "I liked playing for Walter Alston," he says, sitting back in the booth. "He was a good manager. But I think he was a little senile at times. There were times during the 1970 season he put Pee Wee Reese's name on the lineup card. And Reese has been retired now fourteen, fifteen years. He put Charley Neal's name in the lineup. One time he tried to get our pitching coach to get Ron Perranoski and Bob Miller up in the bullpen. Both those guys had been gone for about three years. Miller was with Chicago, and we're getting killed one night, and Alston said, 'Get Miller warmed up.' 'Skip, he's on the other team.' 'Oh, all right, get somebody up.'

"It was funny, 'cause I was sitting next to him when that happened. Another time, he put Len Gabrielson [pinch hitter, reserve outfielder] at short, and I batted leadoff for him as a pinch hitter. I led off the game as a pinch hitter. But Alston played the game like a chess player. He had his moments. We all get forgetful at times and mess up people's names. But these were sort of funny. He had periods like that."

I enjoy the anecdotes, but I need to ask him about 1971, about the rest of his career. After 1970 he was never a regular again. He says he had trouble regaining the confidence he felt during 1970.

He nods his head slowly. "Yeah. The next spring was probably the worst thing that ever happened to me. Al Campanis had asked Monte Basgal, a coach with the Dodgers, on the second or third day of spring training, to report to one of the other fields with Bill Russell and Bobby Valentine. And I was told that instead of third base, I was going to be playing second. And they said, 'We want to work on double plays.' This didn't make sense. You take pitchers, they don't start throwing nine innings right away in spring training. They start out easily, throwing every third day about the middle of January. They do a lot of running. You got to slowly work up to it. You don't want to hurt that shoulder or elbow. Now, we don't throw nearly as much as pitchers, so you're not gonna go out and do any more than they would. Here the second or third day of training, and the guys at short and third are doing nothing but taking ground balls and flipping them to me at second, then I'd have to throw the ball across my body to first."

He stands and pantomimes the second baseman's pivot and throw. "And we did this for close to an hour and I was exhausted. This was the equivalent of a pitcher throwing seven innings the second or third day of training. I could feel it right here." He touches his shoulder and winces, recalling the pain of eighteen springs past.

"Jim Gilliam came by just as we were quitting and he said, 'What're y'all doing?' I said we were doing double plays. He said, 'Who the hell told y'all to be doing this?' 'Hey, I was just told to come over here.' And he went and told Alston. Gilliam told me right after that workout, 'You're not gonna be able to lift your arm tomorrow.' And he was right. And I'm still kind of resentful, because there was a whole career right there. They tried to say I hurt myself sliding or falling. But that was a workout that should never have occurred. And basically I'm out for the year. The next day I could not touch my back pocket. I went to surgeons all over the country. And a doctor in Pittsburgh told me it was all in my mind. Anyway, I was really ticked off. I knew I couldn't throw. And that night, after the game, I went into the clubhouse and I don't think I ever drank that much that quick. I got myself as drunk as I could, and I went back out there. Field crew was out there and I threw to one of the clubhouse boys.

"And I made myself throw, as much as it hurt, hoping it would loosen up a little. I threw about ten minutes, and about three days later there was a pool of blood beneath the surface of the skin, running all the way down to my hip. So I called the doctor, but nothing was done until the end of the season, when Dr. Frank Jobe operated on my shoulder."

He is looking down, his hands folded on the table before him. Perhaps he, like me, is contemplating the career that might have been. "Aah, there was a year-and-a-half layoff there. And I've never seen anybody come back after a year-and-a-half-to-two-year layoff. I'm happy with my position now, but there isn't anybody who wouldn't still like to be playing, and I guess I think because of that day my career was shortened. It was a field of dreams, though, while it lasted."

It didn't last long. In 1971, he batted only seventy-seven times, mostly as a pinch hitter, and his average tumbled to .225. He repeats that he was not a good pinch hitter. "I liked right-handed pitching. They had better control. I never liked hitting left-handers, which makes no sense. But the only times I'd get to pinch-hit was against left-handers. My lifetime average was much better against right-handers than left-handers."

Still experiencing pain in 1972, Grabarkewitz appeared in just fifty-three games for the Dodgers in 1972, batting .167. Following that season, he and Campanis argued over salary—a difference of only $500. Grabarkewitz chuckles without mirth and shakes his head. "I told him if I'm not worth that additional five hundred dollars, trade me. And he did. I went to the Angels, but I never liked being traded from the Dodgers."

A marginal roster player during the next three seasons, Grabarkewitz bounced from the Angels to the Phillies to the Cubs, and finally to Oakland, where he retired after the 1975 season.

"I left the game because the ankle caught up with me," he says, draining the last of his coffee, waving off the waiter who is offering a refill. "I have a totally fused ankle right now, and I shouldn't even be able to walk without a limp." He stands, and we shake hands. "Yet I can run like a deer." A chortle.

We've been talking for nearly three hours. As we approach the cashier, we make small talk, until, while slipping on his coat, he says, "I got a lot of great memories from baseball, really." He buttons his coat as we stand in line near the cashier. I ask him if he's ever thought about returning to baseball in a coaching or managing capacity.

He shakes his head. "The only job I'd consider would be head of player development for the minor leagues. Other jobs in the game are too political." He pauses. "But you know, there's no gravy train after retirement. The applause ends quickly, and so many of us aren't prepared for it. I was divorced after I got out of baseball, and I think the limbo situation I was in had something to do with that." He is frowning slightly now, but it quickly dissolves into another wide smile. "Hey, this was fun," he says, shaking my hand. He looks at his watch, a man with major responsibilities these days, with appointments to be kept. He walks briskly toward the exit, pivots smartly to his right, moves smoothly outside, snaps his coat collar up, and heads across the parking lot in search of his car.

BILL GRABARKEWITZ'S MAJOR LEAGUE CAREER

Year	Team	Games	Home Runs	RBI	BA
1969	Dodgers	34	0	5	.092
1970	Dodgers	156	17	84	.289
1971	Dodgers	44	0	6	.225
1972	Dodgers	53	4	16	.167
1973	Angels	61	3	9	.163
	Phillies	25	2	7	.288
1974	Phillies	34	1	2	.133
	Cubs	53	1	12	.248
1975	Athletics	6	0	0	.000
TOTALS		**466**	**28**	**141**	**.236**

WES PARKER:

Los Angeles Dodgers, 1970

"I was getting so tired of people saying that Wes Parker was a great fielder but a poor to average hitter . . . that I was just totally determined to prove everybody wrong. I wanted to let people know that I could hit."

To meet Wes Parker is to meet a man sports media types once described as an enigma. His old Dodgers teammate Maury Wills once said, "Wes almost wasn't cut out for baseball." As if to prove it, Parker believes that while he was among the league leaders in most hitting categories in 1970, the effort required to get there wasn't worth the rewards.

Nothing about him suggested a major league baseball career, nor a serious pursuit of any athletic activity. Wes Parker, you see, is a man of culture, of education, of refinement, of Christian beliefs, a man whose interests include classical music, literature, and films—interests that would be considered out of place in virtually any athletic locker room across America from high school through the professional ranks.

Yet from 1964 through 1972, no one played first base better

than Wes Parker. Probably nobody played it as well. He had a career fielding percentage of .996, and once fielded an unheard-of .999—virtual perfection. He spent his entire big league tenure with the Dodgers, setting standards for defensive play at first base that few have approached. He was always given his due for his fielding skills. But in 1970, he became a batter of note as well, hitting .319 and becoming the first switch hitter since Mickey Mantle to drive in a hundred runs. Parker drove in 111—nearly a quarter of his career RBI over nine seasons—and stroked 196 hits, sixty-five more than his previous best. His forty-seven doubles led the majors, and were twenty-three more than he had ever hit before. He was a potent offensive force that year, in effect showing his critics that he was as capable with the bat as he was with his glove.

However, his binge with the bat would last only through 1970. He retired at age thirty-two after the 1972 season with a career average of .267.

Born to millionaire parents, Parker never needed baseball's big bucks, and since leaving the game he's studied acting and landed an occasional role in a film or a TV show. He has also done color for NBC's old *Game of the Week*, and has gotten very involved in investments, which include Disney art and baseball collectibles.

He has agreed to meet me in my small room in a down-at-the-heels motel in Culver City, not far from his residence in Santa Monica.

Wes Parker is fifty now, but looks at least fifteen years younger, retaining the youthful handsomeness that roused bobby-soxers at Dodger Stadium for nearly a decade during his playing days. A lifelong bachelor, he still hopes that marriage is in his future.

On this Friday evening in mid-December, I greet him and direct him to the only chair in the room, while I sit on the too-soft bed and start the tape recorder.

Parker was signed by the Dodgers in 1962, after playing college baseball for Claremont College and USC. He played only one season in the minors, but made three stops that year—Stockton, Santa Barbara, and Albuquerque—before being called up by Los Angeles. "I played nine consecutive years and never went back to the minors again," he states emphatically. "I should point out, having only had one year in the minors, I was really brought up too soon. And I really think that's one of the reasons I had a hard time hitting in the beginning, and why during my first five years I had low averages."

As a rookie in 1964, Parker backed up regular first baseman Ron Fairly and played outfield. He batted 214 times, hit a modest .257, but drove in only ten runs. He became the regular first baseman in 1965, but hit only .238 as the Dodgers captured the pennant. However, he did manage fifty-one RBI. Through the next three seasons, Parker's batting average dipped steadily from .253 to .247 to .239.

But in 1969 he gave indications that he was about to arrive as a legitimate major league hitter. I mention that he seemed to be coming around that season, batting .278 and hitting a career-high thirteen home runs.

He nods, and contemplates my observation. He is a soft-spoken, thoughtful man, hesitant to speak without considering his response. "Yes, I really would have had a similar year in 1969. If you look at the All-Star break, I was hitting .296. But right after the break I had an emergency appendectomy, so I missed three weeks of the season with that. When I came back, I was weak. I had thirteen home runs at the All-Star break, and I finished with thirteen home runs. That's just a point of reference to show you that I would have had a similar season in 1969 if I hadn't had the operation."

I ask what contributed to his turnabout. He would become a feared clutch hitter in '69 and especially in 1970.

He insists on setting the record straight. He's a detailing man, and he needs to give me his full perspective on how he became one of the National League's best batters in 1970. "Well, my first five years were very difficult. I had mechanical flaws in my swing. I had a lack of physical strength. Growing up as a kid, I had lots of allergies. I had asthma. I always had a light upper body. I had small wrists. Here, grab my wrist." He thrusts his right arm toward me, and I easily encircle his wrist between my thumb and middle finger. "See? Now great hitters like Aaron and McCovey had large, strong wrists. I had no upper-body strength. I weighed one-eighty, but most of that weight was in my legs. That's one of the reasons I had trouble hitting. Plus my lack of experience in the minors, and a certain lack of confidence."

Parker screws up his face; he is trying to remember some detail. "Now, I'm not sure, but I think it was in 1969 that Dixie Walker was hired as hitting coach, and he helped me tremendously. He corrected the one mechanical flaw in my swing, and that is I was an uppercut swinger. Prior to then we didn't have a full-time batting coach. So nobody was able to correct it, including myself. That straightened me out physically." That Parker seemed to have benefitted from Walker's coaching while Grabarkewitz maintained the old Brooklyn "people's cherce" nearly ruined him, is not unique to baseball. Witness the number of players who extoll the virtues of a particular manager, while perhaps an equal number excoriate that same manager. Sometimes a coach's personality clashes with that of the player's, hindering useful dialogue between the two. "As far as confidence went," Parker continued, "because I came up too soon, pitchers were blowing me away. I couldn't get around on fastballs in 1964. I was overmatched. And that developed a lack of confidence, at least against the better pitchers—the hard throwers. For me to get over that, it took Tommy Lasorda.

"Tommy was a minor league coach at the time, and a good friend. Al Campanis wondered how to turn Wes Parker into a good major league hitter. Tommy said, 'I can do it.' And he did. He hung around all spring training, talking, telling me why I should be a better hitter than I was. He said I had the physical attributes of eyesight and coordination, and he convinced me I could be just as good a hitter as I was a fielder. He got me thinking positively."

An oh-so-slight frown pulls the corners of his mouth downward for just a moment. His voice takes on a harder edge as he speaks. "I was getting so tired of people saying that Wes Parker was a great fielder but a poor to average hitter. I was so sick of hearing that, that I just totally determined to prove everybody wrong. I wanted to let people know that I could hit. It isn't a question of finding new energy. It's a question of focusing energy and using it more productively. By 1970 I knew every pitcher in the league. I knew exactly what they were going to throw me under any circumstance. I knew all the ballparks in the league, was accustomed to all the hotels, had friends in every city, and was comfortable with the travel. I knew how to pace myself through an entire season. In other words, I finally knew the game inside and out."

A major factor beyond this, Parker tells me, is that he was healthy the entire 1970 season, playing 161 games. He nods as he talks about it. "It was always hard for me to be healthy, but in 1970 I stayed healthy, and I also had the determination and desire to prove a lot of people wrong. Because of that I decided to focus totally just on baseball.

"I gave up a lot of things. I gave up dating completely. Before that I had dated voluminously. And it wasn't that I wasn't getting rest, it was just that it was preoccupying my time. It was interfering with focus. I didn't answer the phone hardly at all, because I didn't want to know anything about leaving tickets for people. That would be distracting and keep me from focusing on the game. So I pretty much became a recluse and a hermit. I eliminated everything I thought would interfere with my concentration."

1970, for Wes Parker, was an odd contradiction: his daily life took on a monastic bent, but he drew considerable media attention at the same time. "Hey, what's happening with Parker? Where'd he learn to hit like that?"

In fact, once Dixie Walker corrected the flaw in his swing, Wes Parker always knew how to hit like that. But he would never come close to replicating his batting feats of 1970, and I ask him if he knew why that was.

His response is immediate. "Sure. After doing that for one season, I decided it wasn't worth it. Now, I had good years in '71 and '72, but I caught colds again. I got sick. I was distracted. I started doing drug talks to kids. I'd hang around the parking lot after ball games hitting fly balls to kids. Leaving passes for people, having girls at the games and going out with them afterwards." He looks straight at me. "Now, some people can do all that and still play good baseball. I can't. The only way for me to be on top like that was to eliminate all distractions. And that's just the way I'm wired up.

"It was a conscious decision on my part that the sacrifices and effort, the amount of energy that had to go into it, was more than I thought it warranted. 1970 was for one season only. I'm glad I did that once, but I wanted to enjoy all aspects of my career, part of which was dating again, part of which was enjoying people. I didn't want to live like a hermit again, and I really believe that's what it would have taken for me to have another year like 1970."

His response amazes me. Professional ballplayers would kill to have seasons such as Parker enjoyed in 1970. No sacrifice is too great to put up potential Hall of Fame statistics. But the sacrifice was more than Wes Parker cared to make. I'm reminded again of what Maury Wills said, that Wes almost wasn't cut out to play professional baseball.

"Now wait," he says, "I just thought of something else. In college I wanted to change my major from business to pre-med. I went to a counselor, and asked what he thought about that. He said, 'Can you get a B average taking physics and chemistry and classes like that?' I thought about it and said, 'Yes.' He said, 'How hard would it be for you to do that?' I said I'd have to give up everything. No dates, no sports, I'd have to study twenty-four hours a day. Then he said, 'Don't do it. It won't be worth that kind of effort.' And my '70 season was like that. It wasn't worth that kind of effort. It was for the one season only. But I decided in '71 and '72 that I wanted a well-rounded life. I wanted to enjoy myself."

He pauses and goes on to explain that during the '70 season he found himself bored often, because he no longer attended movies, read, or watched TV. "Bad for the eyes, Ted Williams used to say." Instead, he slept more, spent more time in bed. "What do you do with the day when you have a night game?" he asks rhetorically. "You usually get up about ten or ten-thirty. You leave for the park about five, five-thirty when you're on the road. So you have about a seven-hour block which is dead time. What do you do? You can't lie around a swimming pool and sun, because it saps your energy. You can't go shopping, because you're on your feet, and your legs get tired. Basically all that was left is what the old-timers used to do, which was sit in the lobby and watch people walk around. There was really not a whole lot you could do if you wanted to devote yourself entirely to baseball. So what I decided in 1970 was that I would spend more time in bed. I'd sleep until about noon instead of ten-thirty, and that extra hour and half not only gave me more rest, but it removed the worry and fret of what to do for the five hours I had before heading for the park. In fact, I started going to the ballpark earlier just to get out there and relax and calm down, and get myself focused on the game."

He smiles slightly. "It worked very well for me. And I also used to do this. I used to take a little ten-minute nap before the game. Not that I fell asleep. Usually I'd lie down in the shower room in Dodger Stadium on towels, and for ten minutes I'd just be quiet. This is maybe fifteen minutes before the game. I'd just think about who was pitching against us that night and how I was going to get hits off him. I'd totally focus, and I'd hear the National Anthem on the radio and I'd get up and get my glove, lace up my shoes, and run right out on the field completely focused."

Parker's power of concentration enabled him to reverse the pitchers' practices of "setting up" hitters. "I used to set up pitchers," he says, grinning. "You hear all the time how pitchers will set up batters for a particular pitch in a particular situation, but I could work just the opposite. In 1970, when I found out who would be pitching against us the next day, I'd think about him the night before. I'd think about him as I was falling to sleep, about how I was going to get hits off him. By the time the game started, I'd already gotten about twenty hits off the guy. I got to the point where I knew those pitchers so well that I could set them up.

"As an example, in one game against Marichal, I knew he'd start me off with something away. He always, always did that. And I said to myself, 'Fine, I'll work for something out there.'" He is standing now, in his left-handed stance, eyeing the vision of Juan Marichal winding up, delivering the pitch. He pantomimes a lunge toward a pitch clearly outside. "I'd be diving across the plate for something like that, and if he'd thrown an inside pitch, he'd have hit me in the back. Now, I know what he's thinking. Any other pitcher would have come back with an inside pitch, but Marichal is so smart that I knew he was gonna go out there again to make sure of what I was doing.

"Sure enough, and it's ball two. So I said to myself, 'Now, he's gonna come inside.' Bases were loaded, and I was a little under the ball, otherwise it would have been a grand slam home run. The right fielder caught it against the fence, so I got a sacrifice fly. But that's what I meant about setting up pitchers. I set him up for that inside pitch. It's just that I missed it by that much." He holds his thumb and forefinger a quarter inch apart. "I did that all season to pitchers, and I don't know if they knew that.

"To me a lot of hitting was concentration. Once you develop

your physical skills and have a good mechanical swing, without major flaws, it's nothing but concentration. And a certain amount of intelligence to guess how a pitcher's going to work you."

Parker, not being blessed with an abundance of athletic skills, had to rely on moxie to succeed at the plate. He was able to do that enormously well for one season. He willed that success to himself. Unlike the truly gifted athletes, for whom batting rudiments come naturally, he had to push himself perhaps beyond his limits to have that .319 season. Yet he was never known as a long-ball threat, hitting only sixty-four home runs in his major league tenure. In 1970, with ten home runs, he nonetheless knocked in 111 runs. How did he manage this with so few home runs?

He doesn't need to think about his answer. "That was a specific goal," he says. "In 1969 I had fifty-seven or fifty-eight RBIs at All-Star break. So I knew I could have gotten a hundred that year without the appendectomy. Therefore when I started the '70 season I said to myself that I was going to knock in a hundred runs. There were two things that I'd never done in my career, and that was to drive in a hundred runs and hit .300. Of the two, driving in runs meant more, because hitting .300 is an individual thing. A hundred RBIs is a team thing, and I was much more interested in team accomplishments. I wanted *us* to win. Some of the bad seasons I had—1966, '67, and '8—by August I had lost my concentration because we were twenty games out. Whenever the team didn't have a chance to win, I pretty much gave up outs. That was another thing I learned in '69 and '70—even if we're behind twenty–nothing in the ninth inning, and I'm up, I try for a hit. But I still could never do as well in those situations as I could when we were tied in the ninth and there were men on base. In fact, there's a book out called *Total Baseball*, and they figured it out that I led the National League in clutch hitting in 1970 and also 1972. I was glad to see that, because I knew I was a terrific clutch hitter. But that never shows in the stats. The reason I was a good clutch hitter was because I just couldn't get involved or excited unless we were in the game." He pauses for a moment, then says, "But I haven't answered your question, have I?"

Unlike many baseball players, Wes Parker is acutely aware of baseball history. He is a fan as well as a student of the game; he remembers other players' stats from years back, and he hearkens to that knowledge in answering my question. "I had the most RBIs with the fewest home runs since George Kell in 1950." That year the Tiger third baseman knocked in 101 runs while hitting only eight home runs. "A big plus for me in '70 was that I batted cleanup, and I had Maury Wills, Billy Grabarkewitz, and Manny Mota batting in front of me, and they all ran pretty well."

I ask him if there are any special memories from 1970, any memorable games or at bats. His response is immediate.

"Yes. During a game against San Diego I got my one hundredth RBI. Manny Mota was on second base, and I'll never understand this. Cito Gaston was playing center field, and I swear to God, if he had thrown the ball home he'd have thrown Mota out. But for some reason, he just lobbed the ball into second after my line drive to center. I never understood why he did that. I hit a bullet, a line drive right at him, and he could have thrown Mota out by twenty feet.

"The other thing was in New York, on the sixth or seventh of May. I had a night where I had a single, double, triple, and home run all in the same game against the Mets. I knew right then and there that I had arrived as a hitter, even though the season was only about a month old. From then on, it was just a different year for me. I got more intentional walks than before. I could feel pitchers working around me sometimes. I never felt that before. Usually they were happy to have me up there, and would come right at me. Now they were nibbling more, trying to make more perfect pitches. I could sense that. Sometimes you could sense fear in the opponent. Not in the great pitchers, of course. But with some of the borderline pitchers I could tell."

He pauses for me while I turn the tape over in my recorder. I ask if he hit well in 1970 against pitchers who formerly got him out easily.

"No." He shakes his head. "Of all the truly great pitchers, the only one who was really hard for me was Marichal. I didn't have any trouble with Gibson or Seaver. I'm not saying they didn't get me out—they did. But I got my hits. I had some big games against Gibson. One game, I got three doubles. Another time I had three for four with a home run. And there was another game where he struck me out four times."

When Parker retired at the end of the 1972 season, only thirty-two years old, he'd led the league in clutch hits, batted a respectable .279, and, if he'd been more like most other major leaguers, could anticipate at least another five seasons in the bigs. Why quit so soon? I ask.

"It was the dead time, hanging around hotels. I'd have liked to have played in Chicago, where they had only day games. Wake up in the morning, go to the ballpark, play the game, go home at night and watch TV or whatever, and have something like a regular life. It's natural, in step with body rhythm of how man was supposed to be: working during the day and sleeping at night. I could never get used to the schedules. It drove me out of my brain. After 1970 I could have retired. The last two years were basically just to be sure I hadn't made a mistake. In fact, I did not. I never, ever regretted stopping when I did."

Yet he went to play in Japan during the 1974 season.

"Yes. They called me right out of the blue and made me a pretty good offer. Paid all expenses and a whole bunch of incentives, and it was a foreign country. I liked Japan and thought I might as well go. I liked it because the things I didn't like about playing here didn't exist there. One thing was reduced travel time. We started at five or five-thirty instead of seven or eight o'clock. You could get up, go to the park, and play your game. Plus they only played a hundred and thirty games, and no trip was ever longer than one hour by train. Games had time limits; doubleheaders had limits. All that cut down on stress and strain. I didn't have to leave passes for people. I didn't talk to reporters, because they didn't speak English and I didn't speak Japanese. They didn't bother me, so I was basically by myself, playing baseball and enjoying life."

Despite what might be called his lover's quarrel with baseball, Parker has never been far removed from it since retiring as a player. He was an NBC sportscaster for seven years on television, and he's done a radio show called *Dodger Talk*, and for four years did *USA Thursday Night Baseball*, until the cable network lost its contract. He coached for the Dodgers in 1984. And he's tried acting as well.

"I did feature films for Billy Graham, and a television series for Norman Lear that was canceled. I've done about forty national commercials, and hosted a health show on TV called *Alive and Well*. I have some talent, but I recognize I'm starting late. I haven't utilized the connections I've made to advance myself as an actor. I don't do the party scene and don't go to the casting people like most actors have to do. So acting isn't what I look to in the future. What I'd really like to do is write a really good baseball novel. I've studied writing, and have gotten some good feedback from professionals who've seen my short stories."

He asks me for some advice on marketing his writing and on locating an agent to represent him, and tells me of his admiration for Ernest Hemingway's novels, especially *A Farewell to Arms*.

Our conversation drifts for a few minutes to the childhood compositions of Mozart, and Parker says he was weaned on classical music, that it was on the radio or phonograph every night during his formative years, and that his grandparents were professional musicians who taught violin, piano, and organ. He chuckles. "If you're a professional baseball player and try to talk to your teammates about Beethoven or Mozart, they think you're some kind of weirdo. But this was part of my upbringing. It was as natural to me as playing baseball."

Were his own teammates aware of that side of him, and did his moneyed background sometimes make it uncomfortable for him in the locker room?

He nods. "Definitely. But you learn to deal with it. When I was at the park, I would focus on baseball. I wouldn't try to talk to these guys about things that didn't interest them. When the game was over I'd go out with other friends who could talk about classical music or Hemingway's writing or great movies.

"Now, I never looked down on the other players. I loved those guys. They taught me so much about being a human being. They taught me a whole other side of life that I wouldn't have seen if I hadn't played baseball. It really rounded out my education. I'll be grateful till the day I die that I had that kind of breadth of knowledge."

The hour is approaching ten, and I've promised the interview would take no more than an hour. We've gone beyond that already, though he seems in no particular rush to move on. Still, I'm intrigued by this man's baseball career, by his apparent absence of frustration over not approaching again his statistics of 1970. But he insists he never experienced that.

"Never felt it. Never. After the 1971 season, when the numbers weren't as good as '70, I wasn't bothered at all. I knew going into the season that 1970 would be my career year."

Finally, I ask him if he missed playing after his retirement, even though I think I can anticipate his response.

"Not one millimeter," he responds immediately. "Baseball, as much as I loved it, was extremely constraining, extremely demanding. And I found I didn't like having to play a baseball game every day for eight months. What I missed is the companionship, the camaraderie, the joking and kidding around. But I still work for the Dodgers in the community relations department. I go out and talk to kids about drugs. I do Christian talks, because I'm a

Christian. I'm also a manager at the Dodgers' fantasy camp." He stands, ready to depart. I start to snap off the recorder, but suddenly he's back playing ball in 1970, and out of the blue, he says, "Physically, I wasn't built to be a power hitter. I learned to hit line drives. That big year I had in '70, I got all those RBIs with doubles, not home runs. I led the league in doubles. Forty-seven. With a runner on third and less than two outs, I think I only failed three times to get that man in all year. I think I was something like seventeen for twenty in that situation." He pauses, steps toward the door, and I turn off the recorder.

I decide that Maury Wills was right, that Wes Parker is not the prototypical athlete; there's the Renaissance man in him waiting to emerge. He's an actor, a writer, a collector of art and rare first-edition books, and he's a man who just happened to flash some of the finest fielding form around first base since Abner Doubleday invented our national game.

As we conclude, bidding our goodbyes, he turns to me at the door and says in afterthought, "I knew I wasn't the strongest ballplayer, or the fastest ballplayer. I also knew I did not have the best throwing arm in terms of power. But I also knew I was intelligent. I knew that since I was, I had to use that to my advantage. And that's what I did in 1970. I learned to think like a pitcher, to break their pitching code. When you can do that, you can guess where that pitch is going to be at better than a fifty, sixty, seventy percent ratio. And if you can do that, you can be a heck of a hitter."

For sure, Wes Parker was, in 1970 anyway, one heck of a hitter.

WES PARKER'S MAJOR LEAGUE CAREER

Year	Team	Games	Home Runs	RBI	BA
1964	Dodgers	124	3	10	.257
1965	Dodgers	154	8	51	.238
1966	Dodgers	156	12	51	.253

Year	Team	Games	Home Runs	RBI	BA
1967	Dodgers	139	5	31	.247
1968	Dodgers	135	3	27	.239
1969	Dodgers	132	13	68	.278
1970	Dodgers	161	10	111	.319
1971	Dodgers	157	6	62	.274
1972	Dodgers	130	4	59	.279
TOTALS		**1,288**	**64**	**470**	**.267**

INDEX

INDEX